/25

God's Prophetic Plan Through the Ages

GOD'S PROPHETIC PLAN THROUGH THE AGES

AN EXPLANATION OF
THE BECKWITH ART CHART
OF
BIBLE HISTORY AND PROPHECY

A Bible Course from Genesis to Revelation

by

GEORGE D. BECKWITH

Author, *The American Home and Character Trends, etc.*

ZONDERVAN PUBLISHING HOUSE
Grand Rapids, Michigan

EIGHT FORTY-SEVEN OTTAWA AVENUE
GRAND RAPIDS, MICHIGAN

To My Wife
ELIZABETH M. BECKWITH,
Whose Faithfulness, Trust, Knowledge of
the Word and Sympathetic Counsel Has
Helped Make This Book Possible;

.   .   .   .

And to the Service of God
In the Church of Jesus Christ.

INTRODUCTION

This is what we might call "The CHART AGE." Business charts, weather charts, etc., are the order of the day. Information travels through "eye gate" as well as "ear gate," and a full mind results when advantage is taken of both means of access to one's inner understanding.

In recent years, "Charts" have come to the front in the pictorial presentation of the Scripture. And without doubt beautiful diagrams greatly aid one's desire for a comprehensive grasp of some aspect of truth.

Of all the Bible charts that I have seen, none has impressed me so much as the "Beckwith Art Chart." It is one of the finest obtainable. Scripturally correct and attractively produced, it is an investment no teacher of the Word will ever regret. For Bible study work, it is unique, and calculated to hold the interest of all concerned.

The designer, George D. Beckwith, is to be highly commended for the most useful key, or explanation, he has prepared. The 25 chapters of his illuminating course of Bible History and Prophecy offer preachers abundant material for a series of messages that will help to stimulate a passion for the Scriptures on the part of their people.

We heartily commend the "Chart" along with its book, "God's Prophetic Plan Through the Ages," praying that the consecrated labors expended in the production of such will stimulate deeper interest in the more sure word of prophecy.

HERBERT LOCKYER, D.D.

Liverpool, England.

The author's chart is available in a larger size for platform use. Size 9 x 3 feet. Printed in 8 colors. Price $20.00. Extra copies of the small 18 x 6 inch chart are available at 50c each.

PREFACE

"For other foundation can no man lay than that is laid, which is Jesus Christ" (I COR. 3:11).

"If any man will do His will, he shall know of the doctrine, whether it be of God, or whether I speak of myself" (JOHN 7:17).

* * * * * * *

The foundation theme upon which the Beckwith Art Chart is built is salvation from sin, through the cross of Jesus Christ. Jesus Christ entered into an atonement for sin, big enough to include the last sinner. Countless thousands of people have proved that the blood of Jesus Christ cleanseth from all sin. "Wash me in the blood of the Lamb and I shall be whiter than snow."

Now let us visualize the very beginning of this chart. First, a large, plain, white canvas, 14 feet 5 inches by 4 feet, was stretched on a wooden frame. Near the center of this canvas was drawn a large cross, which was painted blood-red representing the cross of Jesus Christ. Over the cross was placed this reference, 1 Cor. 3:11. Out from the cross in all directions, all the other drawings on the chart were developed.

It is very significant that this cross was drawn and painted on "Good Friday," the anniversary of the crucifixion of Jesus Christ, our Savior. As the student studies the Bible more and more, he will realize that the books of the Bible, which precede the story of the cross, lead up to the cross as the center of the Bible theme; and that the books of the Bible which follow the story of the cross point back to the cross.

On Easter Sunday, just two days after this "Good Friday," there was added to the canvas the open tomb, and the Resurrection of Jesus Christ from the grave. Thus, on

Easter Sunday, there appeared alone on the chart, the cross, the open tomb, and the resurrection.

This chart and this book are made possible because of the combination of four things in the experience of the author, —some experience in drafting gained as an engineering student at Syracuse University; some knowledge of painting; a lifelong interest in the study of the Word of God; and the inspiration and direction of the Holy Spirit. The author feels that this chart and this book are true to Scripture. They are presented humbly and prayerfully with the hope and belief that they will be a blessing to many who already are children of God; and that they will be used, under the direction and power of the Holy Spirit, in the conversion of many yet unsaved. "The secret of the Lord is with them that fear Him; and He will show them His covenant" (Psa. 25:14).

Many Bible references are given both on the chart and in this book. The Scofield Reference Bible gives to the student many connecting references, comments, and summaries.

A number of large copies of this chart, 9 feet by 3 feet, have been made in colors for the use of Bible students and teachers.

GEORGE D. BECKWITH

Gloversville, N. Y.

CONTENTS

CHAPTER I

THE BIBLE—THE WORD OF GOD

"Study to show thyself approved unto God, a workman that needeth not to be ashamed, rightly dividing the Word of Truth" (II TIM. 2:15).

"Thy Word have I hid in mine heart, that I might not sin against Thee" (PSALM 119:11).

* * * * * * *

The Bible is the Word of God and the Word of truth. It is the message of God to man. It is man's only perfect and authoritative rule of life and conduct.

"The Word of God is quick and powerful, and sharper than any two-edged sword" (Heb. 4:12). Its pages are pages of power. Today men must get back to the Bible.

The Bible reveals that the evil that is in the world today is the result of unbelief; that it is the result of the self-will of lost individuals who are blinded by Satan and who are living in sin; that it is the result of man's disobedience to the commands of a holy and all-wise God.

Man's disobedience to the will of God is causing millions to continually separate themselves from God. Millions of men are being lost in sin and death because of lust. "When lust hath conceived, it bringeth forth sin; and sin when it is finished, bringeth forth death" (James 1:13-15).

Organizations of sinful men are controlling our national governments. They are breaking all the laws of God and of the state that make for peace and that hold civilization steady. Sinful men are taking counsel together against the Lord. The hearts of sinful men are failing them, in these days, because of fear, and for looking after those things which are coming on the earth. The Psalmist, in the second Psalm, describes God's judgment on

13

sinful men that take counsel together against Him, when he says, "He that sitteth in the heavens shall laugh; the Lord shall have them in derision. Then shall He speak unto them in His wrath, and vex them in His sore displeasure."

The Bible is the only book that can give a satisfactory explanation, and a clear understanding, of the cause and the meaning of the turmoil and the fear of these troublous times; and it is the only book that can give the remedy for this turmoil and fear. The Bible is the only book that reveals Jesus Christ, the Saviour of mankind.

The Bible tells us of the fact of sin, of the state of man while in sin, of man's doom as a lost sinner, and of God's plan of redemption from sin unto Eternal Life. "For God hath not given us the spirit of fear; but of power, and of love, and of a sound mind."

The Bible is not an ordinary book. To those who have no faith in God, the Bible is a closed book; but to us who believe, it is the inspired Word of God, and the only up-to-date book in the world.

Ulysses S. Grant said concerning the Bible, "Hold fast to the Bible as the chief author of your liberties; write its precepts on your heart, and practise them in your lives. To the influence of this book, we are indebted for the progress made in civilization, and to this we must look as our guide in the future."

William McKinley said, "The more profoundly we study this wonderful book, and the more closely we observe its divine precepts, the better citizens we will become, and the higher will be our destiny as a nation."

Dwight L. Moody, when he was asked from whence he had obtained such lasting power and strength in his life, said, "I have power insomuch as my soul is saturated with the Word of God."

The apostle Paul wrote, "I charge thee therefore before God, and the Lord Jesus Christ, who shall judge the quick and the dead at his appearing and his kingdom; preach the Word; be instant in season, out of season; reprove, rebuke, exhort with all longsuffering and doctrine, For the time will come when they will not endure sound doctrine; but after their own lusts shall they heap to themselves teachers, having itching ears; and they shall turn away their ears from the truth, and shall be turned unto fables. But watch thou in all things, endure afflictions, do the work of an evangelist, make full proof of thy ministry" (II Tim. 4:1-5). Paul says also, "Men shall be lovers of their own selves, covetous, boasters, proud, blasphemers, disobedient to parents, unthankful, unholy, without natural affection, truce-breakers, false accusers, incontinent, fierce, despisers of those that are good, traitors, heady, high-minded, lovers of pleasure more than lovers of God, having a form of godliness but denying the power thereof: from such turn away" (II Tim. 3:2-5).

True Christians humbly believe the teachings of the Word of God. Let us, as servants of God, launch out into the deep: into the deep of God's Word; into the deep of the atonement; into the deep of God's Will; into the deep of the Holy Spirit, where we lose ourselves and our sorrows in the calmness and peace of His everlasting presence.

Because the Bible is the Word of God and the Word of Truth, it has stood the test of centuries. The feeble efforts of a few non-Christian, evil-possessed writers, to discredit the Word of God and to claim that the Bible is a fraud, have been of no avail. Millions of people, both in this nation and in other nations, have received guidance, courage, power and joy from its pages of power.

The Bible is called the Book of books. All of its 66 books are united into one book. The Bible is composed of the very best literature in the English language. It has always been the best book used by parents in the home for the instruction of children and young people. The teachings of the Bible have combined as a powerful influence to make a social order in which right-thinking and right-living shall be the rule.

The Bible has the distinction of being the first book to be printed by John Gutenberg, the reputed inventor of printing. The time of this printing was from 1450 A. D. to 1455 A. D.

The first complete translation of the Bible into English was made by John Wycliff in 1382 A. D. The first printing of the English Bible was made in 1535 A. D., according to the translation of Miles Coverdale, the English translator—over 400 years ago.

Today there are 21,000,000 copies of the Bible, or portions of the Bible, being printed in one year, by 21 different Bible Societies, in nearly 800 different dialects and languages. Statistics show that annually more copies of the Bible are being sold than of any other 100 books combined.

The history of the American Bible Society, one of these 21 different Bible Societies, is very significant. The American Bible Society was organized in 1816 A. D. in the Board of Estimates room in the City Hall of New York City. After 125 years of service, which ended in May, 1941, this society held its 125th annual meeting in this same room.

The record shows that the American Bible Society, during this 125 years of service, has distributed a total of 305,555,700 Bibles and portions of the Bible. This number averages 4 copies of Scripture distributed each minute of the 24 hours of each day of the entire 125 years.

At the present time, the American Bible Society alone is printing in one year over 7,000,000 copies of the Scripture and portions of the Scripture. This is a remarkable record, and one which is an inspiration to all people who are interested in the spread of the Gospel. Thousands of people in the world today will testify, personally, to the importance of this wide distribution of the Word of God, because of the saving and transforming power of the Word of God in their own lives.

The Bible should be read by all men. It should be read slowly, frequently and prayerfully. It should fill the memory, guide the feet, and rule the heart. Wherever the Bible goes, it does good.

"So shall My Word be that goeth forth out of My mouth: it shall not return unto Me void, but it shall accomplish that which I please, and it shall prosper in the thing whereto I sent it" (Isa. 55:11).

Chapter II

GOD—IN THE BEGINNING—THE CREATOR—GOD'S LOVE

"I am Alpha and Omega, the beginning and the ending, saith the Lord, which is, and which was, and which is to come, the Almighty" (Rev. 1:8).

"I am the Almighty God; walk before me, and be thou perfect. And I will make my covenant between me and thee" (Gen. 17:1-2).

* * * * * * *

There is but one living and true God. He is pictured on the Art Chart as the Alpha and the Omega, the beginning and the ending. God is spoken of in the Bible as the Almighty, the Lord God, the Lord Jehovah, the Most High God, the Everlasting God, the Eternal God, and the Lord of Hosts.

God is the Creator of the universe. In the beginning, He created all things, and without Him was not anything made that was made. This creation goes back to the dateless past.

God first created the heaven and the earth. The earth, after the creation, was made void. It is thought that the evil one must have raised havoc on the original earth. God later restored the earth, which bears marks of a cataclysmic change as the result of divine judgment during the pre-historic ages. See Jer. 4:23-26; Isa. 24:1; Isa. 45:18.

God created animal life and human life. He created man that He might have fellowship with him. All through the ages, God has tested man's love for Him. God wants to be enthroned in the heart of man. He has great love for man, and He wants man to love Him.

God is a personality. He is continually on His throne. He is the same God yesterday, today, and forever. He is the eternal God of love.

God is a trinity. There are three persons in the unity of the Godhead: the Father, the Son, and the Holy Spirit. All three were present at the baptism of Christ: the Spirit appeared, the Father spoke, and the Son was baptized.

God is a spirit. He is everywhere. He is omniscient. He is omnipotent. "The heavens declare the glory of God; and the firmament showeth His handiwork. Day unto day uttereth speech, and night unto night showeth knowledge. There is no speech nor language where their voice is not heard" (Psalm 19:1-3).

Man's trust in God is the only cure for the worry and fear that are so prevalent in the world today. Along with trust in God go health and strength. "Then trust in God through all thy days; fear not, for He doth hold thy hand." Also, He is our refuge and strength. A child of God must have faith and confidence in God each day of his life, while he labors in the will of God in peace and happiness. The three elements of success are faith in God, faith in self, and faith in others. With this threefold faith or confidence, a man can put enthusiasm into his work, for enthusiasm is confidence in action. "In quietness and in confidence shall be your strength."

Our country cannot ignore the plain teachings of the Word of God. We in America must recognize our dependence upon God. Without Him, America would never have come into existence. Without Christ, America can be nothing, and can do nothing. Without God, America cannot endure, nor can democracy stand. We, the people of America, must know God, we must search the Scriptures, and we must know the everlasting truth of the Word of God. "Except the Lord build the house, they labor in vain that build it; except the Lord keep the city, the watchman waketh but in vain" (Psalm 127:1).

"They that trust in the Lord shall be as mount Zion, which cannot be removed, but abideth for ever" (Psalm 125:1).

CHAPTER III

THE SEVEN PERIODS OF TIME, OR DISPENSA-TIONS—THE COVENANTS

"God that made the world and all things therein . . .
And hath determined the times before appointed"
(ACTS 17:24, 26).

* * * * * * *

To study the Bible dispensationally is all-important, if one would learn how to divide aright the Word of Truth. God's plan of redemption in the Bible cannot be fully understood except through an understanding of these dispensations.

A dispensation is a period of time during which God tests man in regard to man's relationship to Him. In each period of time there is some revelation of the will of God, and a new test of man. Each dispensation begins in fresh divine light and inspiration, and ends in darkness, gloom, and judgment.

There are seven dispensations, known as: Innocence, Conscience, Human Government, Promise, Law, Grace, and Kingdom. Five of these periods have already passed into history; the sixth is the one in which we, the Church, are living now; and the seventh will follow a period of time called the Tribulation period.

Each new dispensation is introduced by an agreement or covenant between God and man, which originates with God. These covenants are to be fulfilled by man under certain stated conditions. They contain a promise by God to man. God has made eight covenants with man, which are:

1. The "Edenic" covenant, given to Adam and Eve in the Garden of Eden. It was conditioned on obedience (Gen. 1:28-30; 2:15-17).
2. The "Adamic" covenant, given to Adam and Eve after their disobedience to God. It was unconditional (Gen. 3:14-19).

3. The "Noahic" covenant, given to Noah after the flood. It was unconditional and covered all of the people (Gen. 8:20-9:17).
4. The "Abrahamic" covenant, given to Abraham. It was unconditional. It was confirmed to his son, Isaac. It was confirmed also to Isaac's son, Jacob (Gen. 12:1-3; 26:1-5; 28:10-15).
5. The "Mosaic" covenant, given to Moses after the Exodus at Mt. Sinai (Ex. 20:1-26; 21:1-24:18; 25:1-40:38).
6. The "Davidic" covenant, given to King David (II Sam. 7:4-17).
7. The "Palestine" covenant, given to Israel, and conditioned on Israel's repentance (Deut. 30:1-10).
8. The "New" covenant. It was made with Israel, was unconditional, and will cover the period following the Revelation of Jesus Christ and the return of Israel to Palestine (Matt. 26:28-29; Jer. 31:31-37; Heb. 8:7-13).

You will notice on the Art Chart that each period ends with a crisis. At the end of each of the first four periods of time, the crisis is pictured in a rectangle at the top of the period. These crises are known as the Expulsion, the Ark, the Tower of Babel, and the Passover. The crisis at the end of the fifth period is the Cross, at the end of the sixth period the Second Coming of Christ, and at the end of the seventh period the Great White Throne and the Renovation of the Earth by Fire.

Most Bible students of prophecy feel today that the Age of Grace in which we are now living is rapidly drawing to a close. They observe the prominent abnormal economic, social and religious world conditions prevailing, and the peculiar events happening in and around nations, which point to an approaching crisis. It has been observed by thinking people that always a crisis comes to both men and nations when they reach the end of their resources.

Most Bible students agree in the belief that our God is ready again to personally intervene in the course of world events in order that He may definitely change the course of history, and bring judgment upon individuals and nations.

We who know the Word of God are not left in darkness concerning coming events. We analyze them daily in the light of the Bible, and we prepare to meet them with thanksgiving and rejoicing.

In view of this knowledge of the Word of God as imparted by the Holy Spirit, Bible students are convinced that the business of "Getting Right With God" is of first importance to every individual. They observe that the most valuable possession of every Spiritual Christian is a knowledge of the fact of his own salvation from sin and Satan through the cleansing blood of Jesus Christ, the Saviour of mankind; and a realization of his own personal guidance by the indwelling Holy Spirit.

By "Getting Right With God," an individual becomes a member of the mystic body of Christ, which is the Church. He becomes prepared for the future without fear of coming events. He is ready and watching for the Rapture. He is prepared to appear before the "Judgment Seat of Christ" for the judgment of his works done on the earth, and for the reward of the "Crowns" which will be his. Then he will be one of the group called the "Bride of Christ" at the "Marriage Feast of the Lamb," for he will be like Jesus. He will be one of the "Hosts of Heaven" with Christ at the time of His "Revelation"; and he will reign with Christ after the "Tribulation Period" in the "Kingdom Age" when Christ sits on the "Throne of His Father, David."

May all those who study these periods of time be prepared in this "Age of Grace" to partake of the glories of the future life which are in store for all those who love God.

CHAPTER IV

THE PERIOD OF INNOCENCE

"And God blessed them, and God said unto them,
Be fruitful and multiply, and replenish the earth, and
subdue it" (GEN. 1:28).

* * * * * * *

The first period of time is called "The Period of Innocence," as shown on the Chart. It extends from the creation
of Adam and Eve to their expulsion from the Garden of
Eden.

Adam was created in the image of God and he had close
fellowship with God. During this period, he was innocent
of any transgression of the laws of God for he had no
knowledge of good or evil. He was created for the purpose
of companionship with God.

God said unto Adam, "Behold, I have given you every
herb bearing seed, which is upon the face of all the earth,
and every tree, in the which is the fruit of a tree yielding
seed; to you it shall be for meat" (Gen. 1:29).

And God planted in the Garden of Eden the tree of life,
and the tree of the knowledge of good and evil. "And the
Lord God took the man, and put him into the Garden of
Eden to dress it and to keep it. And the Lord God commanded the man, saying, Of every tree of the garden thou
mayest freely eat; but of the tree of the knowledge of good
and evil thou shalt not eat of it; for in the day that thou
eatest thereof thou shalt surely die."

God gave Adam and Eve an existence on earth under the
most favorable circumstances. The hills, the valleys, and
the plains, which were covered with herds of cattle and
with flocks of sheep were theirs. God saw everything that
He had made for man, and behold, it was "very good."

God made his first covenant with Adam. It included
seven requirements which were:

1. Replenish the earth.
2. Subdue the earth.
3. Have dominion over the animal creation.
4. Partake of a vegetable diet only.
5. Till the soil in the garden.
6. Abstain from eating of the tree of the knowledge of good and evil.
7. If they disobeyed, physical death would be their punishment.

Satan, who was working in opposition to God's plan for man, came to the Garden of Eden to tempt Eve. He came in the form of a most beautiful creature, a serpent. In tempting Eve, he questioned God's word about the forbidden fruit. He said to the woman, "Thou shalt not surely die." He lied to her, and lured her to eat of the forbidden fruit.

Eve listened, she looked, she desired, she took, she ate. She gave it to her husband, Adam, and he "did eat."

The result was that both Adam and Eve disobeyed God. The eyes of both were opened. They saw that they were naked. They made for themselves aprons of fig leaves. Fearing the voice of God, they hid themselves. Adam placed the blame upon Eve, and she, in turn, blamed the serpent. Nevertheless, they became children of Satan instead of children of God. They were expelled from the garden. God kept Adam and Eve away from the tree of life, because of their sinful condition.

It is wise for Christians not to go to places that are forbidden, so that they will not be tempted by Satan to look, to listen, to desire and to indulge in the forbidden thing.

Eve had met Satan, the most powerful enemy of God and man. Here began the conflict of the ages between the forces of God and the forces of Satan. Satan laid plans to destroy God's plan for man by tempting the woman. The forces of evil have been trying to frustrate God's great plan of redemption for man ever since that time.

God immediately made a second covenant with Adam and Eve, after their sin of disobedience, called the Adamic Covenant. It included a curse and a promise.

The curse was upon the serpent who was created a most beautiful creature. God said unto the serpent, "Because thou hast done this, thou are cursed above all cattle, and above every beast of the field: upon thy belly shalt thou go, and dust shalt thou eat all the days of thy life" (Gen. 3:14). The curse was that the most beautiful and subtle of creatures became a loathsome reptile. This was one result of sin.

The promise was "I will put enmity between thee and the woman, and between thy seed and her seed; and it shall bruise thy head, and thou shalt bruise his heel" (Gen. 3:15). The atonement of Christ, "made sin for us," is intimated here. It was the first promise of a Redeemer. Christ will ultimately conquer sin, death and Satan.

As the result of sin, the state of woman was changed. Her conception was multiplied, childbirth was to be accompanied with pain. Man was vested with the headship, made necessary by the entrance of sin which is discord (Gen. 3:16).

The curse was upon the ground for Adam's sake. "Thorns also and thistles shall it bring forth to thee; and thou shalt eat the herb of the field: in the sweat of thy face shalt thou eat bread, till thou return unto the ground: for out of it wast thou taken; for dust thou art, and unto dust shalt thou return" (Gen. 3:18-19).

"Because thou hast hearkened unto the voice of thy wife and hast eaten of the tree, of which I commanded thee saying, Thou shalt not eat of it: cursed is the ground for thy sake; in sorrow shalt thou eat of it all the days of thy life" (Gen. 3:17). God's promise to Adam was that he would have physical death, and that his body would return to the ground.

The age of innocence resulted in one of the most disastrous failures of natural man. It has affected the entire human race.

CHAPTER V

MAN—HIS CREATION—HIS DEFEAT—HIS VICTORY

"So God created man in His own image, in the image of God created He him: male and female created He them" (GEN. 1:27).

* * * * * * *

Man was created by God in innocency, and in God's own image; and he was placed on earth by God in a perfect environment. God gave man great power and authority on earth, and had fellowship with him. The whole history of mankind is written in man's relationship to His Creator. God wants man to love and to obey Him, and to be spirit-filled. On the other hand Satan, who is the author of sin, and who has caused the defeat of man through sin, wants man to follow him and worship him and to have nothing to do with God, with His Son, Jesus Christ, or with the Holy Spirit. Of great importance to man is a knowledge of the Bible truths about his own creation and about his own relationship to God, and to the Devil.

Man is pictured on the Art Chart in the age of innocence in the form of an equilateral triangle. His created nature is much different from that of the animal. Even after the fall of man, there is still an enormous "gulf" between the make-up of the lowest human being and of the highest beast. The highest beast has no trace of a religious nature. Science has discovered nothing, and has done nothing, to bridge that "gulf."

Man was marvelously created with a threefold nature— a spirit, a soul, and a body. In whatever part of the earth man is born, or from whatever race or color man develops, there is a universal sameness in his bodily structure, and in his response to like instruction and like environment.

26

The spirit part of man's nature is that which knows (I Cor. 2:11). Because man is a spirit, he is capable of God-consciousness, and of communion and fellowship with God. He lives a spiritual life according as he is filled with the spirit of God. He can appreciate God's people, and has a desire to assemble with them. He feels at home with them (John 3:2-8; Psa. 18:28). Because man is created with a spiritual nature, God can lift the man who is bound in sin, even earth's saddest failures, by the way of the cross, to heaven's purity and heaven's glory.

The soul part of man's nature is the seat of man's affections, of his emotions, of his desires, of his love, and of his active will. Because man is a soul, he has a self-conscious life, as distinguished from plant life (Psalm 42:1-6). Man can choose this day what course he desires to take. He can determine to jump on defeat, and to go forward and upward to a life of victory, a life in which he can have fellowship with God.

The body part of man's nature is his physical structure. There are five senses in his body: seeing, hearing, smelling, tasting and feeling. These five senses give man his world-consciousness, for he can see, hear, smell, taste, and feel. Man can keep his body under subjection, and thereby, through the proper use of his senses, obtain great perfection in his relationship to God.

God has given to man the seed from which is created and developed a separate and a new body. God said to man, "Be fruitful, and multiply, and replenish the earth, and subdue it" (Gen. 1:28). God endowed man, at the very start, with the ability to know when and how to get food, and to know how to nourish the body to keep it alive. The Bible specifies plainly certain rules for the care of the body and certain laws of conduct, which keep the body fit for service, and for fellowship with God. What a marvelous development is man, as God causes him to grow, to protect himself from sin and Satan, and to prosper. God pleads with man to put evil out of his soul, and to get right with Him before it is too late.

Paul divides man into three classifications, according to his development toward the perfection of the spiritual man. These divisions are the natural man, the carnal man, and the spiritual man.

The natural man is the Adamic man, unrenewed through the new birth. See I Cor. 2:14; I Cor. 15:44. Satan has him to prey upon and to play upon. The natural man may be learned, eloquent, and fascinating, but the spiritual content of the Scripture is absolutely hidden from him, because his eyes have not been opened by the new birth, and he does not have the Holy Spirit.

The carnal man is the "fleshly" man. Paul uses the word "carnal" for the believer who lives under the power of the Adamic nature and who walks after the flesh (Rom. 8:9). He is known as a babe in Christ, not walking by the Holy Spirit. He is able to comprehend the truth of the Scriptures only in its simplest form. Paul says that it was necessary to feed these carnal Christians only with "milk," as babes in Christ, for he could not feed them with meat, as he would feed spiritual, spirit-filled men.

The spiritual man is the one who has been born again. He has so surrendered himself to God, since his soul was cleansed from sin by the blood of the Lamb, that he is spirit-filled, and is walking in the spirit, in full communion with God (Eph. 5:18-20).

Man's faith should not stand in the wisdom of man, but in the power of God. Many people want to direct God, instead of resigning themselves to be directed by Him. They want to show Him the way, instead of passively following where He leads. Jeremiah prayed, "O Lord, I know that the way of man is not in himself; it is not in man that walketh to direct his steps" (Jer. 10:23). The Psalmist said, "Teach me Thy way, O Lord, and lead me in a plain path" (Psalm 27:11).

New life comes to a person when he realizes the fact of God's power within a spiritual life, as described by Paul in First Corinthians, chapters two and three; when he realizes that the worldly soul who tries to pester the life out of him is but nothing when compared with the power he has when he walks and talks with God. Our success depends upon the working of the hidden spiritual forces within a quiet spirit. God says to man, "Be still and know that I am God." He says also, "Thou shalt worship the Lord Thy God, and Him only shalt thou serve" (Matt. 4:10).

Chapter VI

SIN, SATAN, AND WAR

"Sin is the transgression of the law" (I JOHN 3:4).
"To him that knoweth to do good and doeth it not, to him it is sin" (JAMES 4:17).

"Whatsoever is not of faith is sin" (ROM. 14:23).
"She that liveth in pleasure is dead while she liveth" (I TIM. 5:6).

* * * * * * *

Satan is the author of sin, and the father of lies. He is the one who has been tempting and destroying people throughout all history. The scripture presents him as the Prince of the present world system, and the God of this world. He is at the head of a vast host of demons, who are his emissaries (Matt. 7:22; Matt. 25:41).

Satan is known in the Bible by many different names. He is called Lucifer (Isa. 14:12), Satan (Rev. 12:9), The Prince of the Power of the air (Eph. 2:2), The Devil (Rev. 20:2), The Dragon (Rev. 12:3), Beelzebub (Matt. 12:24), Belial (II Cor. 6:15), Abaddon (Rev. 9:11), Apollyon (Rev. 9:11), The God of this world (II Cor. 4:4), The Serpent (Gen. 3:1), The Antichrist (I John 2:18).

In spite of all these names, we must realize that there is only one true God, the Almighty God, the Creator of man, and of the universe; and that He is on His throne at all times as ruler of the universe. God pleads with man to forsake his sinful ways, to leave the deceitful Satan, and to receive freedom from sin and death through Jesus Christ, the Lamb of God that taketh away the sin of the world, and the one who giveth Eternal Life.

When a man has been delivered from Satan's sinful ways by being born-again, he feels it and he knows it. He knows that he has passed from death unto life; that he has been received as a member of Christ's body, Christ's Church, against which the gates of hell cannot prevail.

Satan is continually trying to work in the lives of godly people in opposition to the power of the Holy Spirit. He is also trying in his own deceitful way to blind the eyes of his own people so that they cannot see and understand that their lives are powerless without first being forgiven and cleansed from sin by the blood of Jesus Christ.

Sin starts to develop in the soul of a man, the seat of his desires, and the home of his will-power. Sin is first detected by the outsider through the sinner's eye, the window of man's soul. The effect of sin spreads in man until it is observed in his speech, that which speaks coming out from the heart. Later, sin is seen in man's whole facial expression, which is a picture of his thoughts. Finally, sin affects man's walk and the action of his whole body. Sin later causes man to be plainly seen as a sinner, and known as a sinner. The Prince of this World becomes enthroned in the heart of a sinner, and claims him as his follower. Jesus Christ is the only one who can break the power of sin and Satan.

Sin in the soul of a man is like dry-rot in an apple, which not only destroys the life of the apple, but spreads to the other apples in the barrel and destroys them also. Good apples must be separated from the bad ones in the barrel in order to preserve their goodness.

The man who has been born-again must not stay in the companionship of sinners; he must have fellowship with Christians. Man in sin knows the right, but he is powerless in his own strength to fight against evil. In order to have power to do the right, he must be cleansed from sin by the blood of Jesus Christ, and separated from Satan by the power of the Holy Spirit.

Jesus Christ is the only Saviour that the world has today, or has ever had. He is the only one who can save sinful man from sin, Satan and death. Also He is the Great Physician who can cure those who will put their trust in Him, in spite of the fact that they may be called incurable.

Satan at first was created as "The anointed cherub that covereth." He was given great responsibility and authority by God. He was the "Guardian Angel" of the "Throne of God." He was a being of beauty, and perfect in all his ways from the day that he was created until iniquity was found in him. He is well described in Ezek. 28:12-19.

Satan's heart was lifted up because of his beauty and his authority. Satan corrupted his own wisdom, and became proud, presumptuous and powerful. He said in his heart, "I will ascend into heaven; I will exalt my throne above the stars of God; I will sit also upon the mount of the congregation in the sides of the north; I will ascend above the heights of the clouds; I will be like the Most High" (Isa. 14:12-17). Feeling his power and authority, he boasted about what he would do.

The selfish "I will" uttered by Satan marks the beginning of sin in the universe. This led him to be deceitful, subtle, fierce, cruel, malignant, and wicked. It led him to revolt against God and the kingdom of God. Satan fell from his high place of authority in the kingdom of God because of this sin.

After the Devil was forced to abdicate his place of authority because of his sin and revolt at the "Throne of God," he made the earth and the air the scene of his subversive activities.

The Lord said unto him, "I will destroy thee, Oh Covering Cherub" (Ezek. 28:16). The Lord made a covenant in which He promised the ultimate destruction of Satan through the seed of woman (Gen. 3:15). God knew that Jesus was to be that "seed." Jesus has already conquered sin and death by His death and resurrection; and He will yet destroy Satan and all his followers, and all his works

(I John 3:8). Jesus Christ while on earth had the power
to cast out demons, and He did so (Matt. 4:24; Matt. 8:16).

The Cross of Calvary is the only place where the defeat
of Satan is a permanent reality in the life of a believer.
That sacrifice of Jesus destroyed all of Satan's legal rights
over man and over the earth, and Satan knows it. Thus
Jesus Christ is the legal owner of the world.

As Christ resisted the Devil and vanquished him, so the
Christian must resist the Devil by the power of the Holy
Spirit. "Resist the Devil and he will flee from you." The
Christian must put on the whole armor of God, that he may
be able to stand against the wiles of the Devil. "For we
wrestle not against flesh and blood, but against principalities
and powers." The Christian must be strong in the Lord,
and in the power of His might (Eph. 6:10-18). Faith in
God is the victory that overcomes the world.

After God had first restored the earth to its primitive
beauty and perfection, and He had declared, "It is very
good," Satan made his second malicious attempt to destroy
the work of God. This he accomplished by beguiling Eve,
the mother of all living. He subtly caused her to question
the authority of the Word of God. This marks the entrance
of unbelief into the world. Jesus said of the Holy Spirit
that when He is come, He will reprove or convict the world
of sin—because they believe not on Me.

Satan first appeared unto Eve, "as an angel of Light."
He appeared in the guise of a serpent. Scofield says, "The
serpent, in his Edenic form, is not to be thought of as a
writhing reptile, for this condition is the effect of the curse
upon the serpent. This creature may have been the most
beautiful creature, as well as the most subtle."

Step by step Eve was led on, first to listen to Satan, then
to look at the forbidden fruit, and then to take and eat.
Paul says, "Adam was not deceived, but the woman being
deceived was in the transgression." Someone has written,

"The woman sinned by allowing herself to question the word of God; and the man fell because of the love God had put into his heart for the helpmeet whom God had formed from his own body." The first Adam fell because of love. He was a type or foreview of the second Adam who came down where fallen man lived, "was made flesh and dwelt among us" (John 1:14), made himself of no reputation, took upon himself the form of a servant, and was made in the likeness of man" (Phil. 2:7). "For He hath made Him to be sin for us who knew no sin, that we might be made the righteousness of God in Him" (II Cor. 5:21).

Thus Satan caused the downfall of the race of mankind, plunging them into sin; but God, in His infinite love and mercy, gave the promise of His one remedy for man's sin, in that the seed of woman should bruise the serpent's head. God's promise of the redeemer to come is fulfilled in Jesus Christ. The Godly line of the Old Testament leads through Seth, Noah, Abraham, Isaac, Jacob, Judah, and David. Here began many promises and prophecies of Jesus Christ which were fulfilled in His birth.

Ever since Satan caused Eve and Adam to fall, he has been going about as a roaring lion seeking whom he may devour. His children are the wicked ones, the sinners (Matt. 13:38; Acts 3:10); they are possessed with the Devil (Luke 22:3); they are blinded by him (II Cor. 4:4); they are deceived by him, (I Kings 22:21); they are ensnared by him (I Tim. 3:7); they are troubled by him (I Sam. 16:14); they do the lusts of the Devil (John 8:44); they will be punished together with him (Matt. 25:41). Through the past ages and up to the present time, Satan has opposed God's plan for man. Jesus would not yield to the power of the evil one, because He knew, as one of the Godhead, the greater power of God. Jesus said to the Devil, "Get thee behind Me, Satan."

Today Satan and his demons are free to tempt and to possess people who will yield to him. Satan now organizes his people on the principle of force, greed, selfishness, ambition, and sinful pleasure; and he names his people with attractive names to deceive God's people. He changes these names at will to deceive.

At any time now, for the time is ripe, Jesus will take His saved ones, His Church, to be with Him. Then Satan will be free from the restraint of the Holy Spirit, to do his havoc with the people on earth in the Tribulation period.

During the Tribulation period there will be war in heaven, and Satan and his angels will be cast out of the lower heavens to the earth beneath by the angel Michael. Then Satan, being on earth, will first attack the Jews, God's Chosen People. He later will give power to the beast. At the close of the Tribulation period, when Christ comes with His Hosts of Heaven to judge the nations, Satan will be bound, and cast into the "bottomless pit," where he will stay for 1000 years, during the Kingdom Age. After the 1000 years, he will be loosed, and he will revolt with multitudes of his people. He will be judged, and will be cast into the Lake of Fire, reserved for him and his angels. Thus God will keep His promise, and Satan will receive his just reward, and will be destroyed. See Matt. 25 :41 ; Rev. 20 :10.

The question is often asked by many people, "Why does God permit the war in which we are now engaged?" These people do not realize that war is a part of the evil that is in the world today; for they do not read and study what is said in the Word of God about sin. They do not realize that man is a sinful and guilty creature, and that sin is being permitted to run free in the lives of men. They do not sense the seriousness of sin, and the consequences of sin. It is the war within people that gets people into war.

Man should realize that there is something wrong in the order of things in the world. He should be influenced by the results of war and destruction to hate sin, to seek to find out why things are wrong, and to turn to God, the creator and preserver of man, for light and understanding.

"If any man lack wisdom, let him ask of God, that giveth to all men liberally and upbraideth not; and it shall be given him" (James 1:5).

God punishes sinful man, and He often uses war to lay open the fact of sin in the world. When people persist in sinning, God destroys such people. He destroys nations also. In Bible history, an invasion was often a Divine punishment for great evils in a nation. God sometimes gave severe orders that none should be spared in battle. All sin and evil will eventually be destroyed.

People who do not know their Bible have also a mistaken conception of God. They think of Him only as a God of love, when in fact He is not only a God of love, but He is a God of justice and a God of wrath, as Bible history firmly convinces us.

God is a God of righteousness, and therefore He is opposed to sin and unrighteousness. He desires that men cease from evil thoughts, and evil ways, and become righteous.

Evil men are behind the turmoil of this dark hour, and behind these men is Satan. Evil men are known to create war to serve their own selfish ends. "For we wrestle not against flesh and blood, but against principalities, against powers, against the rulers of the darkness of this world, against spiritual wickedness in high places" (Eph. 6:12).

"In all these things we are more than conquerors, through Him that loved us" (Rom. 8:37). In the events of life, temptations are important to help settle and confirm us in the spiritual life. Our spiritual conflicts against temptation are among our choicest blessings, for they cause us to dig deeper into God's Word, and to trust Him more. Temptations are to us like winds that cause the mighty trees of the mountains to push down deeper into the soil. Satan is used in our temptation to train us for his ultimate defeat. God tests His children, and Satan tempts them. God never tempts, and Satan never tests.

Through Christ we not only win against temptation, and defeat Satan the tempter, but we capture the enemy and make him fight in our ranks; and we receive many spoils of battle. We become more than conquerors through Christ Jesus.

Chapter VII

THE PERIOD OF CONSCIENCE—THE FLOOD

"And the Lord God said, Behold, the man is become as one of us to know good and evil" (Gen. 3:22).

* * * * * * *

The second dispensation of time is Conscience. It extended from the fall of Adam to the flood, a period of 1,656 years. Conscience is defined as a knowledge of right and wrong. In this period, conscience became man's guide. By its standard, man accused and excused himself. Man's goal was to do all known good, and to refrain from doing evil (Gen. 4:7). Although conscience caused man to know and to fear wrong, it did not provide him with the power to keep himself from doing wrong, for which grace is needed.

The descendants of Adam and Eve in this age multiplied rapidly. They deteriorated rapidly also, as the result of doing wrong for, (a) there was union between the "sons of God" and the "daughters of men": (b) there was great wickedness upon the earth, for every imagination of man's heart was only evil continually: (c) the earth was filled with violence, and was corrupt, for man corrupted his way upon the earth: (d) the people refused to listen to the preaching of Noah, and to his warning of the coming world-disaster.

The age of conscience is referred to as the age of ignorance (Acts 17:30, Rom. 1:20-32). But ignorance is no excuse for wrong doing, and it will not save man from punishment. "For as many as have sinned without law, shall also perish without law; and as many as have sinned in the law shall be judged by the law" (Rom. 2:12). At the close of the age of conscience, punishment came to all sinners alike.

The blood-sacrifice of Abel, and the fruit-sacrifice of Cain are pictured on the Chart in the age of conscience.

God had respect for the blood-sacrifice of Abel because of the blood (Heb. 11:4), but not for the fruit-sacrifice of Cain without the shedding of blood (Gen. 4:5; I John 3:12). Cain was displeased because of this; so, in his sin, he slew his brother, Abel.

Seth was born to Adam and Eve to take the place of Abel in the royal line which leads to Christ by the way of Noah and Shem, as shown in white on the chart. The people of this age were very brilliant but very corrupt. The line of Cain went downward, headed straight for the judgment of the flood.

God in this age had to intervene personally in the affairs of men. A world crisis was about to come because of evil. Noah alone "found grace" in the eyes of the Lord, because he "walked with God." So God revealed to Noah, 120 years before the flood, that He would destroy man from the face of the earth by means of a flood. He revealed also to Noah the plans for the Ark. Noah obeyed God and built the Ark. It was a type of boat which men today are copying. Noah preached to the people and warned them of the coming disaster, but they heeded not. The flood came, and God purified the earth. It was the greatest catastrophe that the world has even seen. All flesh that moved upon the face of the earth died, with the exception of Noah, his wife, and his sons and their wives, together with the creatures in the Ark. A Russian Refugee aviator, Mr. Roskovitsky, has told of the finding of the wreckage of the Ark in a small lake on top of Mt. Ararat, just prior to the Russian Revolution.

Evidences of the flood are seen in different countries, such as China, India and Mexico. Jesus referred to the flood in Matt. 24:37, and in Luke 17:26. Paul mentions it in Heb. 11:7. Peter declares it in I Peter 3:20, II Peter 2:5, II Peter 3:3-6.

As it was in the days of Noah, so shall it be also in the days of the "Son of Man." They ate, they drank, they

married wives, they were given in marriage until the day
that Noah entered the Ark. In doing these things, they
forgot to worship God. The flood came and destroyed
them all (Luke 17:26-27).

After the flood, Noah pleased God by offering a sacrifice. It was here that God made an unconditional covenant with Noah. This is the third great covenant made
between God and man (Gen. 8:20-9:17). The covenant
was:

1. God will not curse the ground any more, nor destroy all the living.
2. Noah and his descendants were to be fruitful, to
   multiply, and to replenish the earth.
3. They were to have dominion as before over the
   animal creation.
4. They could add meat to their vegetable diet, if they
   drained the blood out of the meat.
5. The law of capital punishment was established.
6. The earth should never again be destroyed by
   water. The sign of this covenant was the rainbow.

Before the flood, there was one man, Enoch, who was
in fellowship with God. He was translated to heaven
that he might not see death. Enoch is a type of the
Christian Church, which, because of their faith, will be
translated before the tribulation period (I Thess. 1:10;
Gen. 5:24; II Thess. 1:7). Enoch's translation is shown
on the Chart in the age of conscience by the arrow point-
ing upward.

Noah was preserved during the flood because of his
obedience to God. He is a type of the Jews who go
through the tribulation period. The Ark is pictured on
the Chart at the close of the age of conscience. Under
the Ark is pictured the flood, where the people of the
age of conscience ceased to exist. The bodies of these
people went to a watery grave, and their souls and spirits
went to the place appointed for the wicked dead. The
age of Conscience ended in failure.

Chapter VIII

THE PERIOD OF HUMAN GOVERNMENT—THE TOWER OF BABEL

"And God spake unto Noah, and to his sons with him, saying, and I, behold, I establish my covenant with you and with your seed after you" (GEN. 9:8).

* * * * * * *

The third dispensation of time is the period of Human Government. Noah and his three sons, Ham, Shem and Japheth, were the only men left to start a new civilization. After the flood had settled, Noah offered a sacrifice which pleased God. God made a covenant with Noah, as described in the preceding chapter. Noah was then over 600 years old, and Shem, the youngest son, was 98 years old.

God gave to Noah and to his sons a purified earth on which to live, with ample power to govern it. Their responsibility was to govern it for God. Again, under Human Government, man's relationship to God, his Creator, was tested. This age lasted 427 years, and ended in failure.

God, in His covenant with Noah, told him and his sons to be fruitful and to multiply, and to replenish the earth, but they refused to obey. Instead of covering the earth, they stayed in one portion of the land; they stayed together, under one language, because they chose to remain on the plains of Shinar where the soil was rich. There they attempted to become independent of God.

The Lord's promises to the sons of Noah were definite. He said that the descendants of Ham would be an inferior and servile people (Gen. 9:24, 25). The line of Shem would have a peculiar relationship to Jehovah. Consequently, all divine revelation has come through the Semitic race. The holy prophets were of this race. Christ, in the

41

flesh, descended from Shem (Gen. 9:26, 27). God said that the family of Japheth would be the enlarged race, the Gentile nations, developing government, science and art (Gen. 9:27).

In the age of Human Government, the people sought to make a name for themselves and to forget the commands of God. And they said among themselves, "Go to, let us build us a city and a tower, whose top may reach unto heaven; and let us make us a name lest we be scattered abroad upon the face of the whole earth" (Gen. 11:4). They forgot God's promises, and attempted to guard against another flood.

The results of the age of Human Government were that God determined to intervene personally in judgment; the common language was abolished; the work of building ceased; and the dispersion of the race followed.

Most of the people continued in idolatrous worship. The Adamic and the Noahic covenants, however, continued with the Gentile people after their dispersion.

The history of Babel, meaning confusion, parallels the professing worldly church which will end in a man-made unity of the Papacy and of the numerous sects of Protestantism. Babylon is symbolic of Babel. The age of Human Government, therefore, was a failure, ending in confusion of tongues and in dispersion.

On the chart are listed the sons of Japheth, of Shem, and of Ham. The tower of Babel is pictured at the close of the period. The next period is the age of Promise.

Chapter IX

THE PERIOD OF PROMISE—THE CALL OF ABRAM—THE ORIGIN OF NATIONS THE PASSOVER

"Now the Lord had said unto Abram: Get thee out of thy country, and from thy kindred, and from thy father's house, unto a land that I shall show thee; and I will make of thee a great nation, and I will bless thee, and make thy name great, and thou shalt be a blessing; and I will bless them that bless thee, and curse him that curseth thee; and in thee shall all families of the earth be blessed. So Abram departed as the Lord had spoken unto him" (Gen. 12:1-4).

* * * * * * *

The fourth dispensation of time is called the period of promise. It lasted from the period of self-government to the period of law, 430 years.

Before the age of promise, the people on earth lived as one nation with one language; but after the building of the Tower of Babel, God saw fit to separate the people into different nations, with different languages, because they had disobeyed him, and had become idolatrous children of the Devil (Deut. 32:8). This separation of the people by God caused the origin of nations.

You will notice on the Art Chart, in the age of self-government, the names of the different sons of Ham, Shem and Japheth, who were the sons of Noah. You will notice, also, after the picture of the Tower of Babel, the names of the nations which were given as an inheritance by God to the descendants of Ham, Shem and Japheth.

After the origin of nations, God called out Abram from the family of Terah in the land of Ur of the Chaldees to be the father of a new nation. God wished to use a new and chosen people in His plan for the ages. God made an unconditional covenant with Abram which was confined to the Hebrew race. This covenant or promise is outlined at the bottom of the Art Chart, preceding the diagram of the World Powers.

Abram left the land of his fathers, as God commanded him, to go to the land which God promised him for a heritage. His people were to increase and to become a separate people, the chosen people of God. Abram's name was later changed to Abraham.

The Abrahamic covenant was re-affirmed to Abraham after his faith was tested in his offering-up of Isaac (Gen. 22:15-18). God's covenant with Abraham became an everlasting covenant (Gen. 7:1-8:22). This covenant was wholly gracious and unconditional.

Abraham became dissatisfied after a time. There was a famine in the land and he went from his promised land down into Egypt (Gen. 12:10). While there, he did not call upon God. Later, he returned to his promised land.

God's promise was re-established to Isaac, Abraham's son (Gen. 26:24). It was later re-established to Jacob, Isaac's son (Gen. 28:1-5). The descendants of Abraham became distinctively the heirs of promise, and they had but to remain in their own land to inherit their promised blessings. To this day, they have never claimed all of their promised land. This prophecy must be fulfilled.

Jacob blessed Joseph, the youngest of his twelve sons. Jacob's name was changed to Israel, meaning a soldier of God, after he wrestled with God. Joseph was taken into Egypt where, because he had proved so true in the midst of trouble, he was given great power and authority in the land of the king. Jacob and all of his people went into Egypt at the time of great famine in the land. Joseph was used of God to bless the children of Israel in Egypt. The children of Israel increased mightily while in Egypt. After the death of Joseph, they were sorely oppressed. They lost their blessing by going into Egypt, but they did not lose their covenant.

By the grace of God, Moses, who was led by God to spend forty years of preparation in that country, was raised up by God to be the deliverer of the children of Israel from Egypt. God definitely directed Moses. At the command of God, Moses instituted the passover. The blood of a lamb was sprinkled on the outside door frame of each house in order that the first-born child in that house might be delivered from death by the death angel who was to pass by that house. The passover is celebrated as an important annual event in Jewish history.

By the power of God, the children of Israel were brought out of Egypt. The age of promise ended when Israel exchanged grace for law at Mt. Sinai. The age of promise, as a mode of testing the people, was exclusively Israelitish.

You will notice a diagram on the Art Chart below the age of promise, which shows the start of the different world powers, such as Babylon, Egypt, Assyria, Greece and Rome. This diagram pictures the relationship of these world powers to each other, and also to God's chosen people, the Jews. The nation whose line of progress is at the top of the diagram at any one time is in supremacy during that particular time. The Jewish nation was decidedly affected by the nation in supremacy. The Jewish people were in Egypt while Egypt was supreme. When Babylon was supreme, the people of Judah were captive in Babylon. The Roman Empire was supreme during the life of Christ.

In order to understand the development of nations, one must read his Bible history thoroughly. The Bible is the only book that gives us the right conclusion to the whole matter. God's covenant or promise to Abraham, Isaac and Jacob continues as an everlasting covenant.

Chapter X

THE PERIOD OF LAW

"And the Lord came down upon Mount Sinai, on the top of the mount: and the Lord called Moses up to the top of the mount: and Moses went up" (Ex. 19:20).

* * * * * * *

The fifth dispensation of time is the period of law. This period is a necessary conclusion to the failure of the preceding age, the age of promise, where God allowed men to govern themselves. In this dispensation of law, God Himself proposed to rule His chosen people through His chosen representatives.

The law was given to Moses by God on Mt. Sinai. It was a moral, a civil, and a ceremonial law. It presented to the people a visible plan and place for worship.

The Mosaic covenant was in three parts. The commandments were a ministry of condemnation and of death. They expressed the righteous will of God (Ex. 20:1-26). The judgments governed the social life of Israel, such as: relationship of master and servant, injuries to persons, rights of property, and crimes against humanity (Ex. 21:1-23:1). The ordinances governed the religious life of the people. In the high priest they had a representative with Jehovah; and in the sacrifices they had a "cover" for their sins, in anticipation of the cross (Ex. 24:12-31:18; Heb. 5:1-3; Heb. 9:6-9; Rom. 3:25-26).

The law was in three parts. The first was oral, as described in Ex. 20:1-17. In this oral law there was no provision for a priesthood, or for sacrifice for failure. Judgments were given and instructions outlined for the conquest of Canaan.

The second part of the law was given to Moses when he was called up to the mount to receive the tables of stone. There he received instructions concerning the tabernacle, the priesthood and the sacrifice (Ex. 25:31). While he was up on the mount, the people, led by Aaron, broke the first of the Ten Commandments. Moses, returning from the mount, broke the tables of stone.

The third part of the law was given to Moses when he was called back to the mount, when the second tables were made.

On the Art Chart, in the age of law, you will find pictured the law tables, the tabernacle, the temple, the image of Nebuchadnezzar as interpreted by God through Daniel, the "star" representing the virgin birth of Christ, the period of the life of Christ and the "cross" representing the death of Christ. On the line representing Jewish history, you will observe the exodus from Egypt, the division of the kingdom, the dispersion of the ten tribes of Israel, the Babylonian captivity, and the return of the two tribes of Judah to Palestine.

This age of the law is called also the age of the prophets. It was the age when the prophets prophesied of coming events. 400 years elapsed between the time of the silencing of the voice of the prophets in this age and the voice of John the Baptist who appeared at the end of this age and who cried in the wilderness, "Prepare ye the way of the Lord." Christ, the Messiah, came at the close of this period, not to destroy the law, but to fulfill the law by turning men to serving the living God.

At the close of this period, the Jewish priests and leaders were so engrossed in legalism and in ritualistic sacrifices that they overlooked the prophecies concerning the promised Redeemer; and they rejected Him, their rightful King. God tested His chosen people throughout this entire period. The age of law extended from the exodus at Mt. Sinai to the cross at Calvary. It was followed by the age of Grace, the Church Age.

Chapter XI

THE JEWISH PEOPLE AND PALESTINE

"In the same day the Lord made a covenant with Abram, saying, Unto thy seed have I given this land, from the river of Egypt unto the great river, the river Euphrates" (GEN. 15:18).

* * * * * * *

There was neither Jew nor Gentile before the call of Abram. The chosen people of God whom Abram was directed to lead as a new nation were first called Hebrews. They were known as Jews after the time of Judah. The people of all other nations were known as Gentiles. Thus we had on earth at that time, and have had on earth since the origin of nations, two distinct classifications of people, the Jews and the Gentiles.

The old testament has to do almost entirely with the development of the Jewish people, and with their relationship to the Gentile nations and to God.

Another great classification of people known as the church composed of both Jews and Gentiles was promised by Christ (Matt. 16:18). They are called Christians. The Christians are those people who have become members of the church of Jesus Christ by having faith in God and in His Son, Jesus Christ. They have been born again from death unto life. Both Jews and Gentiles have been baptized by one spirit as Christians into one body in Christ, called the church of Jesus Christ. See I Cor. 12:13, compare Acts 2:1-3, 41-47, Eph. 1:22-23. In the Christian church the distinction between Jew and Gentile disappears. We have now on earth, therefore, three classifications of people, Jew, Gentile, and Christian (Eph. 2:14-18).

You will see by the Art Chart that the Jewish people have outlived all other nations. The Jewish race has existed for about 4000 years. During that time they have had many manifestations of the presence of God. No other nation has ever produced such great men as Moses, Joseph, Elijah, Elisha, David, Isaiah, Jeremiah, Ezekiel, Daniel, Paul and many others.

The Jewish race was raised up by God to teach the fact that there is only one God; to write and to preserve the Holy Scriptures (Rom. 3:1-2); to bring to the world a Saviour, who is Jesus Christ; and to save the world from moral decay.

On the Art Chart, God's covenant with Abraham is outlined. The descendants of Abraham are shown by the central line on the Chart. The Jewish people wandered into Egypt. They returned from Egypt. Then God made a covenant with Moses called the Mosaic Covenant. He gave the law to the people, through Moses. The tabernacle was built. The Jews wandered in the wilderness for 40 years. Later they entered the promised land and the temple was built. They were ruled by judges, then by kings. The kingdom became divided. The Jews observed the law until the destruction of Jerusalem in 70 A. D. The Jewish people disobeyed God, and were never allowed to claim all of their promised land.

God made a covenant with David. He said, "The throne of David shall never be destroyed" (Luke 1:30-33). "Thy house and thy kingdom shall be established forever; thy throne shall be established forever" (II Sam. 7:4-17).

The ten tribes of the Kingdom of Israel were carried captive into Assyria in 721 B. C., as shown on the Chart. They have become a wandering people. The two tribes of Judah were taken captive into Babylon by Nebuchadnezzar. Nebuchadnezzar destroyed the Jewish temple.

Daniel, one of the Babylonian captives, became very prominent in Babylon as a prophet of God. He interpreted the image-dream of Nebuchadnezzar, as revealed by God. He interpreted the hand writing on the wall for Belshazzar. He interpreted also his own vision.

The tribes of Judah, after being in captivity in Babylon for 70 years, returned to Palestine, and rebuilt the temple and Jerusalem. In this rebuilding program they had trouble continually. In 63 B. C. they became subject to the Roman Empire. It was this empire which controlled Palestine at the time of Christ.

The Jews rejected Jesus Christ, their Messiah. They crucified Him. Because the Jews rejected their Messiah, they became a scattered people, without a country. Titus of Rome destroyed Jerusalem in 70 A. D. and the two tribes of Judah were dispersed. Israel is known as a "Hidden Treasure," and it will remain hidden until the "Fullness of the Gentiles" is completed.

Many prophecies concerning the return of the Jews to Palestine and the rebuilding of Palestine are recorded by different prophets. The tribes of Israel and of Judah will go back to Palestine, their former land, as one group, as represented on the Chart. This is prophesied in the vision of "Dry Bones" of Ezek. 37:11, and in the vision of the two sticks which become one, meaning the whole house of Israel. The Jews will go back to their land unconverted. However, they will become converted in Palestine later. "A new heart also will I give you; and a new spirit will I put within you: and I will take away the stony heart out of your flesh, and I will give you a heart of flesh; and I will put my spirit within you and cause you to walk in my statutes; and ye shall keep my judgments and do them. And ye shall dwell in the land that I gave to your fathers; and ye shall be my people and I will be your God" (Ezek. 36:26-28).

God gave Israel, through Moses, the "Palestinian Covenant," as recorded in Deut. 30:1-10. It will go into effect after their return to Palestine, and after their conversion.

The "New Covenant" with Israel is to be made after they go back to Palestine (Heb. 8:7-13; Jer. 31:31-37). It has to do with the finished work of Christ and with Israel's future completeness.

Before the Jews are converted in Palestine, they will be judged during the period of the great tribulation. God will purge the rebels out from among them. The Jews who transgress God's law shall not enter into the land of Israel (Ezek. 20:34-38). The testing of the Jews is called the "Time of Jacob's Trouble." A refuge for the Jews, when the antichrist sets up his image, will be the wilderness countries beyond the Jordan: Edom, Moab, and Ammon (Rev. 13:14-15).

Finally, the Jews will look upon Christ whom they have pierced. They will accept Christ as their Messiah, and the Jewish nation will be born again. Paul said that he, a Jew, was "born out of due time."

In the Kingdom Age, the Jews will possess their land. They will build the temple, and sacrifices will be offered again. The government will be set up. The "Sheep Nations" of the earth will be blessed through Israel. Many will say to the Jews, "We will go with you; for we have heard that God is with you" (Zech. 8:20-23). Jesus will say to the "Goat Nations," "Depart from me, ye cursed, into everlasting fire" (Matt. 25:41). Jesus will be king, and His Church will reign with Him. He will rule on the throne of His Father David. During this time, Satan will be bound in the "bottomless pit," he will revolt with many of his people. This host of "wicked ones" will be devoured by fire which will come down from heaven. "The devil that deceived them was cast into the lake of fire and brimstone, where the beast and the false prophet are, and shall be tormented day and night forever and ever" (Rev. 20:10). The will of God will be done fully on earth after the present order is cleansed by fire, and when there is a new heaven and a new earth.

PALESTINE

The Jews love Palestine, their promised land. Since 70 A. D., the time of the destruction of Jerusalem, this country has been destitute and barren. Now it is beginning to bud, and will "blossom like a rose."

Palestine is in the heart and center of the world. It is a vital connecting link between three mighty continents. It holds a strategic geographical position on the earth. It will be coveted by all nations.

Before the first world-war, the Turks had control of Palestine for many years. In 1917, General Allenby captured Jerusalem from the Turks for Great Britain. As a Bible student, he realized the significance of this capture. Before going into Jerusalem, he dismounted from his horse, removed his hat from his head, and went into the city with bowed head. He went in without firing a single shot, for the Turks did not fire because of General Allenby's name since "Allah" meant God to them.

The land around Jerusalem is very rich. It is so rich that as many as five crops have been harvested from the same soil in one year. Agriculture is rapidly developing in Palestine.

After the capture of Jerusalem, investigations were made of the composition of the waters of the Dead Sea. It was found that the waters of this sea were rich in valuable and needed salts, and that these salts could be removed from these waters through the process of evaporation. It was also found that God had provided clay banks along the Dead Sea that are so arranged that a series of large clay reservoirs could be made at different levels. These clay beds were connected so that when the water from the sea was pumped into the first vat, and the hot powerful sun, through the process of evaporation, had caused the heaviest substance in the water to settle, the remaining water could be run into the next clay vat ready for the same kind of process for the next lighter mineral. The water is continually being evaporated in these clay beds by the hot sun.

For hundreds of years, these valuable substances have been washed from the land round about by the rains and deposited by the streams in the Dead Sea. It is estimated that there are in the Dead Sea from 1200 billions to 1300 billions of dollars worth of salts, such as chlorides, bromides, potash, potassium, and the like. It is estimated that there are 260 millions of dollars worth of bromides which can be used for medical purposes, and 70 billions of dollars worth of potash, which is being put back on the land. Shiploads of potash from the Dead Sea have arrived in America. It is estimated that there are 825 billions of dollars worth of magnesium chlorides in this sea.

God has provided these minerals for use in the time of need, and to help carry out His plan for the future.

Haifi, the great harbor of Palestine on the Mediterranean Sea, has been rebuilt. Ships for carrying oil to other countries are loaded at Haifi. 800 tons of oil refined in Palestine have been shipped. A pipe line 600 miles long has been constructed to run from Bagdad in the land of Iraq to Haifi. 60,000 tons of potash have been produced in one year in Palestine and shipped from Haifi.

Britain's only source for potash and bromides is the Dead Sea. Plans are being made for the building of 125 new factories in Palestine for the production of chemicals, medicines and textiles. The olive-growing industry has increased about one third within two years. Sheep raising and farming are being developed now on a larger scale. A great dam for furnishing electric power for industry and for lighting purposes has been built in the Jordan river. This power construction compares favorably with that at the Niagara Falls. Modern cities have been built, like Telaviv, with modern banks and hotels. Telaviv has a population of 100,000 people. The lands on which these cities are built were a barren waste only a few years ago. On Mt. Scopus a Jewish University has been erected.

Do we wonder that this promised land, laden with wealth and with needed minerals, is being coveted by all the nations of the world?

Many battles have been fought on the plains of Asdrelon for the possession of this country; and there remains still another great battle to be fought there, the battle of Armageddon. At that time, Jesus Himself, will put a stop to war. Then He will come to judge the nations. After that, He will set up His kingdom on earth. Then the Jews who have been converted will govern the nations. Peace and plenty will reign, and the Gentile "Sheep Nations" will prosper and be blessed.

The Jew is the barometer of the future. Already 425,000 Jews are in Palestine. The Jewish exhibit at the World's Fair in New York City was most significant. It showed production and plans for development in Palestine. Many Jewish people in America are making investments in land and industry in Palestine. Surely the "fig tree" is budding.

Many Jewish people have already been converted. They have accepted Christ as their Messiah. A great work is being done in America among the Jews. Their eyes are being opened to the Light. They are remembering what Jesus said while on earth, "I am the Way, the Truth, and the Life." Surely "the house of Jacob shall possess their possessions."

Let us now look a little closer into the conditions under which the Jews will enter the land of promise, as outlined in the Palestinian covenant. The Jews have never as yet taken the land of Palestine under the Abrahamic, everlasting covenant, and they have never possessed the whole land (Deut. 29, 30). This covenant will be fulfilled.

The seven parts of the Palestinian covenant are:

1. Dispersion for disobedience (Deut. 30:1).
2. The future repentance of Israel, while in the dispersion (v. 2).
3. The return of the Lord (v. 3).
4. Restoration to the land (v. 5).
5. National conversion (v. 6).
6. The judgment of Israel's oppressors (v. 7).
7. National prosperity (v. 9).

CHAPTER XII

THE PROPHETS AND BIBLE PROPHECY

> "We have also a more sure word of prophecy; where-
> unto ye do well that ye take heed, as unto a light that
> shineth in a dark place, until the day dawn, and the
> day star arise in your hearts. Knowing this first, that
> no prophecy of the scripture is of any private inter-
> pretation. For the prophecy came not in old time by the
> will of man; but holy men of God spake as they were
> moved by the Holy Ghost" (II PETER 1:19-20).

* * * * * * *

It is for us today to consider present world activities in
the light of Bible prophecy, and in the prospect of future
results. Next to a knowledge of salvation should be a
knowledge of God's prophetic program for the times in
which we are now living.

A prophet is one who speaks forth the message which
has been communicated to him through divine inspiration,
whether of practical duties or of future events. A list of
many Bible prophecies and of their fulfillment is given in
the concordance of the Scofield Reference Bible.

The age of the prophets covers a period of about 500
years. The prophets during this period are (1) pre-exile
prophets: Obadiah (887 B.C.), Jonah (862 B.C.), Joel
(800 B.C.), Amos (787 B.C.), Hosea (785 B.C.), Isaiah
(760-698 B.C.), Micah (750-710 B.C.), Nahum (713 B.C.),
Zephaniah (630 B.C.), Jeremiah (629-588 B.C.), Habakkuk
(626 B.C.). (2) Exile prophets: Daniel (607-534 B.C.),
Ezekiel (595-574 B.C.). (3) Post exile prophets: Haggai
(520 B.C.), Zechariah (520-518 B.C.), Malachi (397 B.C.).

The whole scope of prophecy must be taken into account
in determining the meaning of any particular Bible passage
(II Peter 1:20). The pivotal chapters, taking prophecies

as a whole, are Deut. 28, 29, 30; Psalm 2, and Daniel 2, 7. The key that unlocks the meaning of prophecy is the prediction of two Advents of the Messiah: the first advent to suffering, and the second advent to glory. The devil hates prophecy because he does not want people to know that he and his works are to be destroyed by Christ. He hates the Bible, he hates Christian people and he hates Christ.

One clear proof of the truth of the Bible is the fact that, of all the Bible prophecies, not one has failed to come to pass in its time. The Christian has reason to believe that all prophecies concerning this present day and future days will also be fulfilled in their time, for the Bible is the Word of Truth.

Daniel, the key prophet of God during the Babylonian captivity, said, "And I heard but I understand not; then said I, Oh my Lord, what shall be the end of these things? And he said, Go thy way, Daniel, for the words are closed up and sealed till the time of the end" (Dan. 12:8, 9).

The time of the end is here, because the Holy Spirit is opening the eyes of Christian people to the meaning of these prophecies. There are thousands of Christians who are not surprised or astonished by the present otherwise appalling trend of events. Instead of having their faith disturbed or destroyed, they see the Bible prophecies being fulfilled before their eyes. These people are more interested in the study of God's word, and are more active in His service, because they have increasing hope, as they see the day approaching, "Looking for that blessed hope and the glorious appearing of the great God and our Saviour, Jesus Christ" (Titus 2:13). The remedy for the world chaos is the personal return of Jesus Christ.

A worldly church and a worldly people, who do not fellowship with God, cannot understand the strange events about which they read in the daily newspapers and magazines, and which they hear talked about over the radio and on the street. They are so busy trying to do good that they do not take time to read the prophetic word in the Bible. The wise are those who understand God's book and who teach the same.

Prophecies have a way of becoming history. They pass into history unnoticed by the blind world. But to the Bible student, light and understanding beams suddenly upon particular prophecies in the Bible. As these events pass, only a literal and an exact fulfillment gives this light to students. Bible searchers can praise God that they have been given a knowledge of present and future events in the light of Bible prophecy.

Chapter XIII

THE TIMES OF THE GENTILES

"And Jerusalem shall be trodden down of the Gentiles, until the times of the Gentiles be fulfilled" (Luke 21:24).

* * * * * * *

The Gentile people include all those who are not Jews. Therefore all people are divided into two classifications— Jews and Gentiles.

"The times of the Gentiles" is that period of time which started in 606 B.C., when world power passed into the hands of Nebuchadnezzar, King of Babylon, at the command of God (Jer. 27:1-21); and when Nebuchadnezzar invaded Palestine and led the Jews captive into Babylon, and destroyed the Jewish temple at Jerusalem. This captivity of the Jews was the result of their disobedience to the commands of God and of their falling away into idolatry. "The times of the Gentiles" will last until the Revelation of Jesus Christ.

There is a difference between the period called the "times of the Gentiles" and "the fullness of the Gentiles." The fullness of the Gentiles refers to the complete formation of that group of Gentiles who make up the church of Jesus Christ. This period of time is called the church period. It started with Pentecost and lasts until the Rapture of the church. Paul says in Romans 11:25, "blindness in part is happened to Israel until the fullness of the Gentiles be come in." There has been up to the last few years an exceedingly small number of Jews who believe in Jesus (Romans 11:4, 5). After the Rapture and during the tribulation period, a remnant out of all Israel will turn to the Lord as their Messiah, and will become His witnesses (Rev. 7:3-8). "The fullness of the Gentiles" is the completion of the purpose of God in calling out from among the Gentiles a people for Christ—the Church.

There are four prophets during the Babylonian captivity —Daniel, Obadiah, Jonah, and Nahum—who speak of Gentile world history. Of these four, Daniel is the chief.

Daniel became a mighty prophet because he purposed in his heart that he would not defile himself, and God used him. He was not ashamed to confess God in a strange land. He dared to trust God. He would not compromise with the devil. This is the secret of a great life. God rules over the minds of saints like Daniel.

Daniel became a companion of kings, and he was given great authority in Babylon. He talked with angels. He was recognized as the prince of wise men. God led him to interpret the image dream of Nebuchadnezzar and to interpret his own visions, all of which prophesied the course of the Gentile nations, and "the times of the Gentiles."

The image of Daniel, second chapter, is pictured on the Art Chart directly following the Babylonian captivity. The dream of Nebuchadnezzar and the visions of Daniel, seventh chapter, have a similar interpretation. The image of the dream was composed of four different metals which represented four world empires. Each succeeding metal decreased in value but increased in strength. The four beasts of Daniel's visions, which came up out of the sea, represented the same four world empires of the image.

The Babylonian kingdom was represented in the image by the head of gold, and in Daniel's vision by the beast which was like a lion with eagle's wings.

The Medes and Persians were represented in the image by the chest and arms of silver, and in Daniel's vision by the beast which was like a bear raising itself up on one side and having in its teeth three ribs, representing this threefold dominion.

Alexander's Grecian empire was represented in the image by the thighs of brass, and in Daniel's vision by a beast which was like a leopard which had four heads and four wings on its back, representing the four divisions of the empire.

The Roman empire is represented in the image by the two legs of iron and the feet and toes of part iron and part clay, and in Daniel's vision by a beast which was "dreadful and terrible and strong exceedingly," and which had great iron teeth. It devoured and brake in pieces, and stamped the residue with the feet of it; and it was diverse from all beasts that were before it; and it had ten horns."

The history of the Gentile nations had just passed through the leg period of the Roman empire when the empire was destroyed. The history of the Roman empire did not reach the feet and ten toes period of the image. The ten toes period of part iron and part clay represents the ten-kingdom period of the Roman empire in its final form, the ten toes representing the ten-kingdoms of the Roman empire which have yet to be broken with "the Stone" of Daniel 2:34. "Thou sawest till that a stone was cut out without hands, which smote the image upon his feet that were of iron and clay, and brake them to pieces. Then was the iron, the clay, the brass, the silver, and the gold, broken to pieces together, and became like the chaff of the summer threshing floors; and the wind carried them away, that no place was found for them: and the stone that smote the image became a great mountain, and filled the whole earth" (Daniel 2:34, 35). Jesus is that "Stone" cut out without hands. He will come at the Revelation, and will fulfill this prophecy.

The Roman empire, which was destroyed, must therefore, be revived to close the image dream and to finish the times of the Gentiles. Daniel says so; John says so. Empires rise and fall at the command of God. No man can change God's plan for "the times of the Gentiles" as prophesied in the Bible.

A study of the connecting references given in Daniel and in Revelation concerning the history of the Gentiles as revealed in the image of Nebuchadnezzar, in the visions of Daniel, and in the vision of John, should be followed by the student of the Bible. Thus we look to Bible prophecy which tells us about the close of this Gentile period.

CHAPTER XIV

THE LIFE OF CHRIST—OUR SAVIOUR

"For God so loved the world that He gave His only begotten Son, that whosoever believeth in Him should not perish, but have everlasting life. For God sent not His Son into the world to condemn the world but that the world through Him might be saved" (JOHN 3:16, 17).

"If thou shalt confess with thy mouth the Lord Jesus, and shalt believe in thine heart that God hath raised Him from the dead, thou shalt be saved" (ROM. 10:9).

* * * * * * *

Jesus Christ is the only begotten Son of God. He was conceived by the Holy Ghost, and born of the virgin Mary in Bethlehem of Judea. He is God manifested in the flesh (I Tim. 3:16). He is the second person of the Trinity.

On the Art Chart, the birth of Jesus Christ is represented by a star, and His crucifixion by a cross. After the cross are pictured His resurrection and His ascension.

Jesus Christ was from the beginning. He lived a life of about 33 years on earth. Now He is alive at the right hand of God and He will live throughout eternity.

When Jesus was on earth He had fellowship with God, for He was holy. It was the kind of fellowship that God wants the human race to have with Him. When God created man, He made him that He might have fellowship with him also; but man yielded to temptation, he fell into sin, and he became in need of a Saviour who could bring him back into fellowship with God.

Christ was sent by God into the world on this supreme mission, to be the Saviour of man, to free man from the bondage of sin, and to bring him back to God. Christ came to earth to redeem the lost world from death unto eternal life. He gave His life on the cross to fulfill His mission as the Lamb of God that taketh away the sin of the world. He was crucified, He died, and He was buried.

The third day He arose again from the dead, and thereby He conquered death. He became alive again. He was seen then on earth, after His resurrection, by Mary and by His disciples. He walked with them and He talked with them in His resurrected body for 40 days.

Jesus ascended into heaven where now He is alive at the right hand of God. He is there as our High Priest, "after the order of Melchizedek" (Heb. 6:20). This order refers to the royal authority and unending duration of Christ's high priesthood (Heb. 7:23, 24; Gen. 14:18). Today Christ is making intercession for us, His children. Because He lives, we, who are His, saved by His shed blood, shall live also, when He comes. Christ is coming again to judge the quick and the dead, His Church.

The blind carnal world will never find its way out of darkness until it opens its eyes to a true vision of the mission and power of Jesus Christ: and until it repents of its evil ways, and accepts Him as its Redeemer and Saviour. Jesus is the only one who can redeem this lost world from death unto life. This is the Gospel, the good news of the Bible.

The old testament contains many definite prophecies concerning the birth, life, ministry, death, resurrection, ascension and exaltation of Jesus. Many of these prophecies have been fulfilled, as recorded in the new testament. "And beginning at Moses and all the prophets, He expounded unto them in all the Scriptures the things concerning Himself" (Luke 24:27). Some of these prophecies in the old testament, and their fulfillment in the new testament, are given here:

Prophecy	Fulfillment
Seed of the woman, Gen. 3:15	Gal. 4:4
Seed of Abraham, Gen. 17:7, 22:18	Gal. 3:16
Seed of David, Psalm 132:11	Acts 13:23, Rom. 1:3
Born of the virgin, Isa. 7:14	Luke 1:35
Born in Bethlehem, Judea, Micah 5:2	Matt. 2:1
His public ministry, Isa. 61:1, 2	Luke 4:16-21
His ministry to commence in Galilee, Isa. 9:1, 2.	Matt. 4:12-16
His entry into Jerusalem, Zech. 9:9	Matt. 21:1-5
His zeal, Psalm 69:9	John 2:13-17
Rejected by His brethren, Psalm 69:8	John 1:11-12, 7:5
Betrayed by a friend, Psalm 41:9	John 13:18-21
Sold for 30 pieces of silver, Zech. 11:12	Matt. 26:15
His silence under suffering, Isa. 53:7	Matt. 27:12-14
Spat on and scourged, Isa. 50:6	Mark 14:65, John 19:1
Lots cast for His vesture, Psalm 22:18	Matt. 27:35
His vicarious death, Isa. 53:12	Matt. 20:28
His flesh seeing no corruption, Psalm 16:10	Acts 2:31
His resurrection, Psalm 16:10-11	Acts 2:32
His ascension, Psalm 68:18	Eph. 4:8-10
His exaltation, Psalm 101:1	Heb. 1:3

The eternal Christ is the central theme of the whole Bible. He is of the seed of Abraham and as such, He is the "blesser" of the whole world. The cross on which He atoned for our sins is the fountain of all new life. He is of the line of David, and the one who is heir to the throne of David. He is, therefore, to be Israel's king, "the Desire of the Nations."

Jesus Christ is the Alpha and Omega. He is traced back to God in John 1:1-2 and back to Abraham in Matt. 1:1-17. Jesus Himself traces Himself back to God, "I and my Father are one."

The old testament is the preparation for the advent of Jesus Christ, through its history, its laws, its system of sacrifices and its prophecies. The gospels are the manifestation of Christ in the world. The epistles are an explanation of the gospel of Jesus Christ. The Revelation is the consummation of all the purposes of God in and through Jesus

Christ. In the Old Testament, the New is concealed; while in the New Testament, the Old is revealed.

Christ is the golden thread of victory that runs throughout the entire Bible. Through Christ, the Bible becomes a connected, continuous story of humanity in its relationship to God. Christ, who is the truth, binds together the 66 books of the Bible into one progressive unfolding of the Truth, and with perfect harmony of doctrine.

On the Art Chart, you will notice that Christ was a PROPHET during His earthly life. Now He is our high PRIEST during this church age, the age of grace. He is to be KING during the kingdom age which follows the tribulation period on earth.

Christ will destroy death. "Since by man came death, by man came also the resurrection of the dead. For as in Adam all die, even so in Christ shall all be made alive. But every man in his own order; Christ the first fruits; afterward they that are Christ's at His coming. Then cometh the end when He shall have delivered up the Kingdom to God, even the Father; when He shall have put down all rule, and all authority and power. For He shall reign until He hath put all enemies under His feet. The last enemy that shall be destroyed is death" (I Cor. 15:21-26). This is the Christ who is spoken of in Gen. 3:15 as the "Seed of the Woman." He is the one who is ultimately to destroy the devil and the works of the devil.

The old hymns that we have learned in a Christian home about Jesus and His love, stay with us throughout life.

> "What a Friend we have in Jesus,
> All our sins and griefs to bear!
> What a privilege to carry
> Everything to God in prayer!
> Oh what peace we often forfeit,
> Oh what needless pain we bear,
> All because we do not carry,
> Everything to God in prayer.

"Have we trials and temptations?
Is there trouble anywhere?
We should never be discouraged,
Take it to the Lord in prayer.
Can we find a friend so faithful,
Who will all our sorrows share?
Jesus knows our every weakness,
Take it to the Lord in prayer."

JOSEPH SCRIVEN
CHARLES C. CONVERSE.

"But God, who is rich in mercy, for his great love where-with he loved us, even when we were dead in sins, hath quickened us together with Christ" (Eph. 2:4-5).

Chapter XV

THE GRAVE—THE SOULS OF THE DEAD—
THE RESURRECTIONS

"Marvel not at this; for the hour is coming in the which all that are in the graves shall hear his voice, and shall come forth; they that have done good unto the resurrection of life; and they that have done evil unto the resurrection of damnation" (JOHN 5:28-29).

* * * * * * *

With reference to this chapter, let us direct our attention to the bottom of the Art Chart where are pictured; first, the grave; second, the place for the souls of the righteous dead; third, the place for the souls of the wicked dead; fourth, a great gulf fixed; fifth, the resurrections from the dead.

Many people do not realize that there are separate resurrections of the dead, and that there is more than one judgment. They do not realize that the Bible teaches that there is a long time, a period of 1000 years, between the "second coming" resurrection of the righteous dead, and the "great white throne" resurrection of the wicked dead.

The body of man is the only part of man that dies. The grave is the place on earth where the bodies of the dead, both righteous and wicked, are laid at rest to await their respective resurrections.

The soul of man does not die, but it remains conscious when the body dies, and it goes, after the death of the body, to the place prepared for it. The place for the souls of the righteous dead is called "paradise." It is pictured on the Chart as below the grave before the resurrection of Christ; but it is pictured as in heaven above after the resurrection of Christ.

Christ died, but He arose again and conquered death. When His body arose from the grave, His grave on earth was opened, and His soul and spirit returned from paradise below to join His body on earth. His body was a resurrected body. It was immortal. Christ became the first-fruits of them that slept.

Christ, at His resurrection, led captivity captive. He freed the souls of the righteous dead from paradise below. He closed up the paradise below, and removed it to heaven above. Paul calls the paradise above the third heaven, God's abode (II Cor. 12:1-4). The freed righteous ones, whom Christ brought from paradise below, went to paradise above. This paradise above is pictured on the Art Chart after Christ's ascension. The spirit and the soul of the righteous dead now go to paradise above, and they will remain there until Christ comes to receive His church at the time of the rapture, the time when the bodies of the righteous dead are called forth from the grave.

Under the paradise below, on the Chart, is a great gulf fixed, and under the gulf is the place for the souls of the wicked dead. The great gulf between paradise and hell is impassable.

The story of the "rich man and Lazarus," as found in Luke 16:19-31, shows that the spirits of the departed are conscious; and that they have a "soulish body," which makes them recognizable as they appeared while on earth, for the "rich man" recognized Lazarus and talked with him across the impassable gulf.

The spirit is not without a body after death. The body, soul and spirit of a man can be compared to the make-up of a plum. When the meat or body of the plum dies, it is separated from the stone and the kernel of the plum. The kernel is alive in the stone, its body. The spirit of man is alive in its "soulish" body.

The place in the other world to which the soul and spirit of each person on earth go after death is determined by what each person does with Jesus Christ, the Saviour, whether or not he accepts Christ's sacrificial death on the cross for him and is saved. If sinful man is born-again and is saved while on earth, so that the spirit of God dwells in his heart and he becomes the temple of the living God, then his soul and spirit, after they separate from the body, go to paradise, the place for the souls of the righteous dead. How a person lives as a Christian, determines the rewards or crowns he will receive at the Judgment seat of Christ.

If a man is unsaved while on earth, and evil is enthroned in his heart so that there is no place for God in his life, his soul and body go to the place prepared for the souls of the unsaved, the wicked dead. The saved or unsaved condition of man while on earth determines, therefore, where the departed spirit of man will reside after death, and it determines the time when his body will be resurrected from the dead.

Since Adam, there has been physical death, and there is to be also a physical resurrection. "As in Adam all die, even so in Christ must all be made alive" (I Cor. 15:22). Both are physical.

The first resurrection is the resurrection of the righteous dead. It is in two main parts, as shown on the Art Chart. The first main part occurs at the time of the rapture, when the "dead in Christ" shall rise first, when the bodies of the righteous dead are called out, leaving the bodies of the wicked dead in the grave.

The second part of the first resurrection is the resurrection of the tribulation saints at the close of the tribulation period. The saints are the people who have witnessed for Christ during the tribulation period, who have not worshipped the beast, nor his image, nor have received his mark on their forehead or on their hand (Rev. 20:4). The souls of these tribulation saints are under the altar until the resurrection of their bodies. These saints shall live with

Christ, and serve him day and night in His temple (Rev. 7:15).

The Christians who are alive on earth at the time of the rapture will not see death, for they will go immediately to be with Christ. They have been born twice and do not die at all. People who are born twice and die, die only once. Those who are born only once will have to die twice.

Hades will hold the souls of the wicked dead until the second resurrection, which is 1000 years after the revelation of Jesus Christ. At the second resurrection, the bodies of the wicked dead will come forth from the grave. They will be reunited with their wicked souls, and they will appear before the "great white throne" for their judgment. After this judgment, they will go to the second death, the lake of fire.

The first resurrection is for those who are saved, the righteous dead shall come forth unto the resurrection of life (Eph. 2:8-9). The second resurrection is for those who have done evil, who shall come forth unto the resurrection of damnation (John 5:29). "Blessed and holy is he that hath part in the first resurrection; on such the second death hath no power, but they shall be priests of God and of Christ, and shall reign with Him a thousand years" (Rev. 20:6).

CHAPTER XVI

THE PERIOD OF GRACE—THE CHURCH— THE BELIEVER

"For the grace of God that bringeth salvation hath appeared to all men, teaching us that, denying ungodliness and worldly lusts, we should live soberly, righteously and godly in this present world; looking for that blessed hope, and the glorious appearing of the great God and our Saviour, Jesus Christ" (TITUS 2:11-13).

* * * * * * *

This Age of Grace is the age in which we are living today. It extends from the Cross of Calvary to the Second Coming of Christ.

The Grace of God is defined by Paul as, "The kindness and love of God, our Saviour, toward man" (Titus 3:4); and "His kindness toward us through Jesus Christ (Eph. 2:7). He saved us not by works of righteousness which we have done, but according to His mercy. "For by grace are ye saved through faith; and that not of yourselves: it is the gift of God" (Eph. 2:8). "The Grace of God is God's unmerited favor granted to unworthy sinners who have nothing in themselves to commend themselves to God." "Being justified by his grace, we shall be made heirs according to the hope of eternal life" (Titus 3:7).

Dr. C. I. Scofield says that the grace of our Lord Jesus Christ saves, justifies, builds up, makes acceptable, forgives, redeems, bestows an inheritance, gives standing, provides a throne to which we may come boldly for mercy and help, teaches us how to live and gives us a blessed hope. "Let us therefore come boldly unto the throne of grace, that we may obtain mercy and find grace to help in time of need" (Heb. 4:16). Jesus says, "My grace is sufficient for thee."

The age of grace is a marvelous age because it is the age of the Gospel of the grace of God. This age follows the age of law. Let us compare the age of grace with the age of law.

The age of law is known as the Jewish age, while the age of grace is the Christian age, or Church age. The Jewish law and grace do not intermingle, for law is God-prohibiting while grace is God-bestowing. Law is that which shuts up, but grace is that which opens up. Law brings condemnation to the best, while grace brings justification to the worst. The law curses and kills, but grace forgives, redeems and makes alive. Law leads to a spirit of hatred, but grace leads to love, peace and praise.

Of course there have been both law and grace since the time of Adam: but during the age of law, the law, as given by Moses, was predominant; and during the age of grace, grace and truth which come from Jesus Christ are predominant (Luke 23:43; Rom. 5:15; I Tim. 1:15; I Cor. 6:9-11).

Jesus Christ came at the start of the age of grace to fulfill the law of God. The Psalmist speaks of the law of God in Psalm 1:2, when he says, "But his delight is in the law of the Lord; and in his law doth he meditate day and night."

The law was added to the government of man because of man's transgression. God gave the law to Moses to bring guilty man a knowledge of his sin. "As many as are of the works of the law are under the curse" (Gal. 3:10). "By the deeds of the law there shall no flesh be justified in his sight: for by the law is the knowledge of sin" (Rom. 3:20). "The strength of sin is the law" (I Cor. 15:56).

Man is justified not by the works of the law, but by the faith in Jesus Christ (Gal. 3:26). The law is not of faith (Gal. 3:12). "But after that faith is come, we are no longer under a schoolmaster" (Gal. 3:23-25). "Walk in the spirit and ye will not fulfill the lusts of the flesh" (Gal.

5:16). Paul says to the believer, "For sin shall not have dominion over you, for ye are not under the law but under grace."

This age of grace is a marvelous age, because it is the age of the Church of Jesus Christ. The Church is the living body of Christ, the organism of which He is the living and eternal head. Jesus Himself said, "I will build My Church." It is a most valuable experience to be a member of that great company of believers who have been redeemed by His own precious blood.

The Christian Church means the "called-out" ones, whether they are Jews or Gentiles. Today, in this Church Age, both Jews and Gentiles, who are saved, may be partakers alike of the promises of God for the Church. God is miraculously "calling-out" His people from among all nations. These "called-out" people must be born-again, and be baptized with the Holy Spirit. This is the mystery of the Church.

The age of grace is a marvelous age, because it is the age of the Holy Spirit. Every saved person receives the Holy Spirit. Every person who comes into the world as a babe is by nature a child of wrath and dead in sin, he is raised up from his dead nature only by the new-birth. This is the new-birth which cancels the spiritual death inherited from Adam, and which begins a spiritual life in Christ Jesus in the believer. God plants the Holy Spirit within these His people the moment they believe in the sacrifice of Jesus Christ on the cross for their sins, and in His resurrection from the grave, and are saved by accepting Him, their Saviour.

This age of grace is a marvelous age, because it is preeminently the age of evangelism. Its outstanding objective is the salvation of souls. To be an active member of a group of people in the Church of Jesus Christ who are making a business of evangelism is a blessed thing.

The purpose of this age of grace in God's plan of redemption is the gathering-out from among the nations the Church of Jesus Christ, against which the gates of hell and Satan cannot prevail. These gathered-out ones compose one body, the Church; they possess one spirit, the Holy Spirit; and they are built upon one foundation, which is Jesus Christ, our Saviour.

The worldly church of today is failing to meet modern needs and to save modern life, because it has failed to recognize the secret of the wisdom and power of the Holy Spirit in this age of the Holy Spirit. Without the Holy Spirit the church is hopeless. Men in the worldly church may have energy and enthusiasm to help humanity, but with no spiritual or lasting results. The carnal mind does not understand, for it has no contact with the Holy Spirit. It is the spirit that quickeneth. The lamps of the carnal man possess no oil, which is the Holy Spirit. Without oil they will not be ready when the Bridegroom cometh.

The so-called modern churches are still on Satan's side of the conflict. They are busy trying to do good without spiritual help. They are not born-again unto eternal life. Rev. 3:1 says, "I know thy works, that thou hast a name that thou livest, and art dead." Satan, the deceiver, is posing around these churches as the angel of light, and his ministers are posing as ministers of righteousness, but ignoring the Holy Spirit. Satan is always inventing new religions without the aid of the Holy Spirit, religions which appeal to fallen human nature as a substitute for being born-again. The chief features of Satan's church are idolatry and priestcraft, things which God hates.

The church needs to see Jesus, and to know Him, its only Saviour. The church needs to see Jesus in the lives and actions of Christian believers.

Every regenerate being in this age of grace is the possessor of two natures; the one nature is received through natural birth, and is hopelessly bad; while the other nature, the new nature, the nature of God Himself, is received through the new-birth, and is wholly good.

Dr. C. I. Scofield says that God does not say that those who do not have the new nature are not refined, or cultured, or able, or sweet tempered, or generous, or charitable, or religious; but He does say that not one of them is righteous, or understands God, or obeys God, or pleases God or seeks after Him.   Unregenerate people are untouched by the sacrifice of Jesus Christ, and they reject Christ's word. They are often filled with sympathy for all the woes and for all the aspirations of humanity, and they are strenuous in their assertion of their human rights, but out of the heart of the unregenerate man "proceed evil thoughts, adulteries, fornications, murders, thefts, covetousness, wickedness, deceit, lasciviousness, an evil eye, blasphemy, pride, foolishness; all these things come from within and they defile the man" (Mark 7:21-23).

"But the natural man receiveth not the things of the Spirit of God; for they are foolishness unto him; neither can he know them, because they are spiritually discerned" (I Cor. 2:14). "Because the carnal mind is enmity against God; for it is not subject to the law of God, neither indeed can be. So they that are in the flesh cannot please God" (Romans 8:7-8).

A Christian has two natures.   He receives the divine nature by regeneration just as he receives human nature by natural generation.   The believer still has his old nature. Regeneration is a creation, not simply a reformation.   It is the bringing in of a New Nature, not the changing of an Old Nature.   Nicodemus was a moral, religious man, but Jesus said unto him, "Except a man be born-again he cannot see the kingdom of God" (John 3:3). "For ye are all the children of God by faith in Jesus Christ" (Gal. 3:26).   On the contrary, if ye do not have faith in Jesus Christ, ye are none of His.   Unless a person is born-again into the family

of God, he has no right to call God his father. The fatherhood of God and the brotherhood of man are not universal.
"For by grace are ye saved, through faith; and that not of
yourselves; it is the gift of God: not of works, lest any man
should boast" (Eph. 2:8-9). Cf. Gal. 3:6, 6:15. All members of the church of Jesus Christ have been born again,
and they are brothers in Christ Jesus, and God is their
Father (I Peter 2:9-12). The Fatherhood of God is found
only in the church of Jesus Christ.

"Therefore, if any man be in Christ, he is a new creature:
old things are passed away; behold, all things are become
new" (II Cor. 5:17). "I am crucified with Christ; nevertheless, I live; yet not I, but Christ liveth in me; and the
life which I now live in the flesh I live by the faith of the
Son of God, who loved me and gave himself for me" (Gal.
2:20). "For ye are dead, and your life is hid with Christ
in God. When Christ, who is our life, shall appear, then
shall ye also appear with Him in Glory" (Col. 3:3-4). "He
that hath the Son hath life, and he that hath not the Son of
God hath not life" (I John 5:12).

However, the two natures, the old nature and the Divine
nature, exist together in the believer. Between these two
natures there is a conflict, as there has been conflict
throughout the ages—a conflict between God and the devil
for possession of the souls of men. The flesh and the spirit
are contrary the one to the other. The young convert, as
well as the old convert, who often depends upon his own
will-power, has trouble to understand life because of this
conflict. The power of the Holy Spirit is the only thing
that can help settle this confusion. "If ye walk in the spirit,
ye shall not fulfill the lusts of the flesh" (Gal. 5:16).

The age of grace is the Church age. The Church of
Jesus Christ is invested with eternal life. This organism
had its origin in the mind of God, before the foundation of
the world, but started after the ascension of Christ. It is
shown on the Art Chart in the Age of Grace as starting

at the time of the descent of the Holy Spirit and continuing on earth until the Rapture. The Church of Christ is not of earth but of heaven (Eph. 1:3). Her members are pilgrims and strangers in this world.

On the Art Chart are shown the names of the seven churches of Asia, as described in Rev. 2:1 to Rev. 3:22. A book by L. Sales Harrison, entitled "The Wonders of the Great Unveiling," gives a clear picture of these seven churches. The letters to these seven churches give a chronological, prophetic picture of the seven periods of the dispensation of the church, and they give also a sevenfold message to the Church. The seven stars on the Chart above the churches represent the messengers of the seven churches (Rev. 1:12-16). John saw our blessed Lord standing in the midst of the churches clothed as a high priest. "His eyes as a flaming fire," and "His feet like fine brass"; both of these expressions are symbols of judgment. "Seven stars were in His right hand." They represent messages. "Out of His mouth went a sharp two-edged sword," a symbol of execution of judgment.

In these seven messages, the Lord said to everyone of the churches, "I know thy works." In these messages, He describes a preview of the conditions as they exist during the seven successive periods of the present Church age.

The Church of EPHESUS, 95 A.D., is described in Rev. 2:1-7. Ephesus means "desirable." It describes the love of the Lord for His church. The Lord condemns this first Church for leaving its first love and for forgetting the Holy Spirit. The message is "To him that overcometh, I will give to eat of the tree of life which is in the midst of the paradise of God."

The Church in SMYRNA, 95-315 A.D., Rev. 2:8-11, represents the martyr period under the Roman Empire. It was threatened with great suffering. Attempts to crush the church were made by ten different rulers. The promise was,

"Be thou faithful unto death and I will give you a crown of life."

The Church in PERGAMOS, 315-500 A.D., Rev. 2:12-17, means "marriage" and "elevation." Before this, the church was in the world but not of it. Now the world married or came into the church. Priesthood was begun; and the church came into imperial favor. The message was "To him that overcometh I will give to eat of the hidden manna; and I will give him a white stone, and in the stone a new name written which no man knoweth save he that receiveth it."

The Church in THYATIRA, 500-1500 A.D., Rev. 2:18-29, means "sacrifice" of the mass and "continual sacrifice." The source of the papal order which makes Mary the queen of heaven is from Babylonian idolatry. Read this description of the papacy in Rev. 2. "As many as have not this doctrine, and which have not known the depth of Satan (or sin), as they speak, I will put upon you none other burden. But that which ye have already hold fast till I come." The promise is "I will give him the Morning Star."

The Church in SARDIS, 1500-1800, Rev. 3:1-6 means "things remaining." There was a reformation in this period, but only a few remained undefiled. The promise is "He that overcometh, the same shall be clothed in white raiment and I will not blot out his name out of the book of life, but I will confess his name before My Father and before His angels."

The Church in PHILADELPHIA, the 19th century, Rev. 3:7-13, means "brotherly love." This is the Missionary Age. The history of Christian missionaries, their aims, their sacrifices, their adventures, their victories, their devotion to the cause of the church of Jesus Christ, is most uplifting and inspiring. Active in spreading the gospel during this missionary age of the church were such men as David Livingstone, who possessed the nobility of self-sacrifice while exploring the dark continent of Africa in the hope of emancipating the black man's soul. There were Sir Henry M. Stanley and Alexander Mackey, and Bishop James Hannington the lion-hearted, all in Africa. There was David Brainerd who labored among the Indian tribes of the North American forests. There was John Williams who sailed among the coral islands of the Pacific to save the souls of men of those islands. There was J. Hudson Taylor of the China Inland Mission, a man full of the Holy Ghost and of faith, with rare power in prayer, with marvelous organizing faculties, with energetic initiative and with influence with men. Hundreds of such men can be mentioned as having been powerful workers in the cause of the Christian church during the Missionary Age, all of which goes to prove that God can work at all times through the lives of humble, consecrated, ordinary, self-sacrificing, faithful men and women.

With this Missionary Church, the Lord finds no fault. The promise is "I have set before thee an open door and no man can shut it." "Him that overcometh will I make a pillar in the temple of my God."

The Church in LAODICEA, the 20th century church, Rev. 3:14-22, means "people's rights." It is the people's church of the present day. It is not the Lord's church. People everywhere are demanding their rights. The Lord stands outside of this church and knocks. He stands at the door of the heart of each individual and knocks to be admitted, for the latch is on the inside.

The Laodicean church of today is lukewarm. It is the people's church without the power of the Holy Spirit. It precedes the Rapture.

The twelve discs on the Chart in the oval above the churches represent the twelve kingdom parables as described in Matt., chapters 13 to 28.

The Lord's supper is pictured above the church. The Lord's table is mounted on wings. One wing points toward the cross, to "show forth the Lord's death." The other wing points to the Rapture, "till He come." "As oft as ye eat this bread and drink this cup ye do show forth the Lord's death till He come." These wings also represent the verse of Isa. 40:31, "But they that wait upon the Lord shall renew their strength; they shall mount up with wings as eagles; they shall run and not be weary; and they shall walk and not faint."

In this present age of grace, the church age, Satan's forces in the world are working against the church of Jesus Christ. Today, we are living in the last period of the church age. The earthly church as a whole does not have the Holy Spirit. There is trouble everywhere in the church and outside of it. This points to Christ's second coming as being near at hand. Bishop J. C. Ryle said "I believe it is for the safety, comfort, and happiness of all true Christians to expect as little as possible from churches or governments under the present dispensation; to hold themselves ready for tremendous convulsions and changes of all things established; and to expect their good things only from Christ's second advent." This is true wisdom. It is the only true optimism. "My soul, wait thou only upon God; for my expectation is from Him" (Psalm 62:5). The age of Grace will end with the second coming of Christ.

Chapter XVII

THE HOLY SPIRIT

"Not by might, nor by power, but by my spirit, saith the Lord of hosts" (ZECH. 4:6).

"And when the day of Pentecost was fully come, they were all with one accord in one place. And suddenly there came a sound from heaven, as of a rushing mighty wind, and it filled all the house where they were sitting. And there appeared unto them cloven tongues, like as of fire, and it sat upon each of them. And they were all filled with the Holy Ghost and began to speak with other tongues, as the Spirit gave them utterance" (ACTS 2:1-4).

* * * * * * *

The Holy Spirit is the third person of the Trinity—the Father, the Son, and the Holy Spirit—as pictured at the very top of the Art Chart. He is from the beginning.

During the time of Old Testament history, the Holy Spirit came upon godly men, and He was wonderfully active through them. The work of the Holy Spirit was then creative, directing and energizing. His manifestations were occasional and special. The Old Testament expression is that "the Holy Spirit came upon" men. The Holy Spirit came from heaven to direct the lives of such men as Enoch, Noah, Job, Abraham, Moses, Daniel, Isaiah, Elijah and Elisha. In the book of Isaiah, 41:10, the Lord said, "Fear thou not for I am with thee; be not dismayed, for I am thy God. I will strengthen thee, yea, I will help thee; yea, I will uphold thee with the right hand of my righteousness."

Later on, when Jesus was here on earth, He talked with His disciples about the Holy Spirit. He told them that He Himself must go away, and after that the Holy Spirit would come to them, to remain in them, His church. (See John 14:17). He said "It is expedient for you that I go away, for if I go not away, the Comforter will not come unto you; but if I depart, I will send him unto you" (John 16:7). The descent of the Holy Spirit to the church, therefore, depended upon the ascension of Jesus Christ. This descent is pictured on the Art Chart in the age of Grace following the ascension of Jesus Christ. Jesus, while on earth, knew that He must go away to take His place at the right hand of God where He is now. He knew that He was to be our High Priest, after the order of Melchizedec to make intercession for us, His followers.

Jesus ascended into heaven as He said, but before He ascended He performed the great mission of His life. He gave His life a ransom for many. He became a sacrifice by giving His shed blood. He was the Lamb of God that taketh away the sins of the world. He had such great love for us that He atoned for our sins. "Greater love hath no man than this, that a man lay down his life for his friends" (John 15:13).

Jesus arose from the grave. He became the first-fruits of them that slept. He conquered sin and death and He is alive now and forevermore. We accept Him as our Saviour by believing in Him. "Believe on the Lord Jesus Christ and thou shalt be saved, and thy house."

Jesus Christ sent the Holy Spirit, the Comforter, after His ascension, as He said He would do. He sent him at the time of Pentecost, to dwell within His disciples. The Holy Spirit was what Jesus told His disciples He would be, an advocate, His representative to dwell within His people. The Holy Spirit is Christ without the limitations of the flesh and of the material world. He did what the limitations of the flesh could not do. Thus Calvary opened the fountain from which was poured forth on the disciples the blessings of Pentecost.

Jesus said, "I will build My Church." This Church was begun at Pentecost. The Holy Spirit came as an advocate of Christ to build the Church, Christ's bride, to direct the

Church, and to remain within the Church as long as it remains upon earth, or until the Rapture. The Holy Spirit came to earth to convict the world of sin. He came to convince the world of righteousness and of judgment.

At Pentecost, the lives of the disciples there assembled were transformed by the Holy Spirit. A new power went to work in the throne of their hearts. Fear was gone. They spoke the truth.

Jesus said to His disciples while He was on earth "But the Comforter, which is the Holy Spirit, whom the Father will send in my name, he shall teach you all things, and bring all things to your remembrance, whatsoever I have said unto you" (John 14:26).

The Bible tells, in Acts 4:31, 33 of another group of people who received the Holy Spirit. "And when they had prayed, the place was shaken where they were assembled together, and they were all filled with the Holy Ghost, and they spoke the Word of God with boldness, and with great power gave the apostles witness of the resurrection."

The Christian church today should be filled with the Holy Spirit. He dwells in the bodies of the believers, for they are the temples of the living God. He instructs the believer and inspires him to prayer which must prevail. The Holy Spirit can reveal what Christ could not speak. He quickens our mortal bodies. He gives health at the same time that He gives life. He makes possible to the believer sufficient energy and strength for a greater work. When the Christian is filled with the Holy Spirit, he receives the gift of power. Men today can be transformed by Him into humble, powerful witnesses for Christ. A person without the Holy Spirit cannot do the work of Christ, for his life is powerless.

The Holy Spirit is the Spirit of God, the Spirit of Truth, but also the spirit of conviction, the spirit of witness, the spirit of power, the spirit of life, the spirit of holiness, the spirit of help, the spirit of adoption, the spirit of wisdom, the spirit of liberty, the spirit of meekness, the spirit of promise, the spirit of love, the spirit of grace, the spirit of revelation, the spirit of prophecy, the spirit of a sound mind, the spirit of glory. In the fullness of the Spirit, there is abundance of wisdom, of resources, and of power.

The Spirit-filled man is God's own perfect model for our lives. Such a person is close to God. He loves to commune with God. There he finds his thorough preparation and power for service. There may be many fillings with the Holy Spirit, but there is only one baptism.

There are many different kinds of places where Spirit-filled men and women have different kinds of experiences while alone with God. Every believer must have time alone with God. This communion with God may be in one's room or in his study or out in the garden or in the orchard or in the beautiful woods. It may take place in the early morning or in the evening twilight while on the still lake alone in a boat or a canoe. It may be up on the lofty mountain top or down along the quiet seashore or by the mighty ocean, that emblem of majestic decision. "If thou wouldst understand thyself, send the multitude away." It is in solitude, alone with God, that we catch the mystic notes that issue from the soul of things, and become surcharged with power divine. "Into the woods my Master went" but out of the woods my Master came, prepared for service.

The gifts and functions of the Holy Spirit are many.

1. The Holy Spirit is the author of the new birth (John 3:5, 6).
2. He was sent by Chirst from the Father (John 15:26).
3. He is the gift of the Father (Neh. 9:20).
4. He is sent in the name of Christ (John 14:26).
5. He testifies of Christ (John 15:26).
6. He was given upon the exaltation of Christ (Psalm 68:18).

7. He imparts the love of God (Rom. 5:3-5).
8. He is given for instruction (Neh. 9:20).
9. He imparts hope (Rom. 15:13).
10. He dwells forever with the saints (John 14:16, 17).
11. He teaches the saints (John 14:26).
12. He edifies the church (Acts 9:31).
13. He sanctifies the church (Ezek. 37:28; Rom. 15:16).
14. He is the Comforter of the church (Acts 9:31).
15. He was given through the intercession of Christ (John 14:16).
16. He is the source of wisdom (Isa. 11:12).
17. He is given in answer to prayer (Luke 11:13).
18. He strives with sinners (Gen. 6:3).
19. He is given according to promise (Acts 2:38-39).
20. He is given to those who repent and believe (Acts 2:38).
21. He is given to those who obey God (Acts 5:32).
22. He regenerates the believer (Romans 8).
23. He is given to the Gentiles (Acts 10:44, 45).
24. He is received through faith (Gal. 3:14).
25. He is an evidence of union with Christ (I John 3:24).
26. He is given as a pledge to the continued favor of God (Ezek. 39:29).
27. He guides into all truth (John 16:13).
28. He reveals the things of Christ (John 16:14).
29. He directs our path (Acts 16:6, 7).
30. He searches all things (Rom. 11:33, 34).
31. He teaches saints to endure and answer persecution (Mark 13:11).
32. He creates and gives life (Job 33:4).
33. He helps our infirmities (Rom. 8:26).
34. He appoints and commissions His servants (Isa. 48:16).
35. He directs where to preach (I Cor. 2:13; Acts 16:6, 7, 10).
36. He instructs what to preach (I Cor. 2:13).

37. He directs the decisions of the church (Acts 15:26).
38. He enables ministers to preach (I Cor. 12:8).
39. He spoke in and by the prophets (Acts 1:16).
40. He reveals the future (Luke 2:26).
41. He is the source of miraculous power (Matt. 12:28).
42. He baptizes all believers into one body, the church (I Cor. 12:13).
43. The world cannot receive Him (John 14:17).
44. It is not by might nor by power but by my Spirit, saith the Lord of Hosts (Zech. 4:6).

The emblems of the Holy Spirit are several—a dove (Matt. 3:16); fire which illuminates, purifies, and searches (Matt. 3:11); oil which consecrates, heals, and purifies (Psalm 45:7); rain, which refreshes and fertilizes; a seal which authenticates and makes secure; a voice which guides, speaks, and warns (Isa. 6:8); water which fertilizes, refreshes, cleanses, and is freely given (John 3:5); wind which is powerful, is independent, and revives (John 3:8).

There is strife, and always has been, between the Holy Spirit and the spirit of evil, the devil. The one is contrary to the other. The flesh guided by the devil lusteth after the spirit, and the spirit after the flesh.

The Spirit leads heavenward. The fruits of the Spirit are love, joy, peace, longsuffering, gentleness, goodness, faith, meekness, temperance; with a dividend of assurance, strength, security, unselfishness, victory, happiness, understanding, satisfaction, encouragement, holy ambition, good influence, happy homes and heaven eternal. If we are led by the Spirit, we are not under the law. On the contrary, the flesh leads downward and profiteth nothing, as it follows the evil one. The works of the flesh are adultery, fornication, uncleanness, lasciviousness, idolatry, witchcraft, hatred, variance, emulation, wrath, strife, seditions, heresies, envying, murders, drunkenness, revelings, and the such (Gal. 5:17-21). They that do these things shall not inherit the Kingdom of God. "The natural man receiveth not the things of the spirit of God: for they are foolishness unto him: neither can he know them, because they are spiritually discerned" (I Cor. 2:14).

The mind of man when apart from the mind of God is inefficient, unsteady and powerless. Human philosophy may seek the solution of the basic problems of life by man's own power, but it still does not give man the power necessary to solve these problems. Man cannot by the senses perceive the non-perceivable, nor by the reason know the unknowable. Man's mind is only bewildered by great mysteries, and in need of wisdom.

Man always knows what he ought to be, and he knows also that he has always fallen far short of his goal. What he needs now is not more light merely, but more power. Man alone is oppressed and weighed down by great sins. He is in need of forgiveness, deliverance, and freedom from sin. Slaves of sin are not free.

Human philosophy may be true, and the greatest of the mental interests of man, but it never can be adequate to bring man into the haven of peace with God and power with man. The feeble light of human wisdom cannot look into the inscrutable future or explore the dark recesses of the human heart. The history of human thought shows that the world by wisdom knew not God.

Peace and power are found in Jesus Christ. The Holy Spirit makes known great mysteries with such simplicity that the newly born Christian can grasp them and apply them. Believers are forgiven for sin through Jesus Christ, for "there is none other name under heaven given among men whereby we must be saved" (Acts 4:12). What man needs is to know the almighty Lord who forgives, and who transforms man's life and enables him to be perfect as his Father in heaven is perfect. Freedom then is no more an unsolved problem, for through the miracle of grace the saved man has been emancipated from the law of sin. The law of the spirit of life in Christ Jesus hath made him free from the law of sin and death. Then, the mysteries of life that have perplexed man in all ages have received their final solutions through the Holy Spirit.

Faith rests in a knowledge of Jesus Christ. Man must know Him. The church must explore the resources of the Holy Spirit. The Church must search the Scriptures. God hath revealed life unto us by His Spirit for the Spirit searcheth all things, yea the deep things of God and maketh them clear unto us (I Cor. 2:10).

God can and He will use a church whose people and pastor are Spirit-filled. Any church today, as in past years, which falls short of this high ideal of life will miss its high calling, however pretentious its claims or however elaborate its organization. Unfortunately, the modern church of to-day is becoming a man-managed, world-annexing, priest-pretending church, and as such it cannot please God. It can never save the world from sin and fulfill the mission of Christ. The modern church is weakening in its spiritual power. In fact, it is gradually declining in its spiritual birth-rate. The true church of Jesus Christ is Spirit-filled. God wants such a Church today. "Let this mind be in you which is in Christ Jesus."

Chapter XVIII

THE SECOND COMING OF CHRIST

"Let not your heart be troubled; ye believe in God, believe also in me. In my father's house are many mansions; if it were not so I would have told you. I go to prepare a place for you. And if I go to prepare a place for you, I will come again and receive you unto myself, that where I am there ye may be also" (JOHN 14:1-3).

"Ye men of Galilee, why stand ye gazing up into heaven? This same Jesus, which is taken up from you into heaven, shall so come in like manner as ye have seen him go into heaven" (ACTS 1:11).

"For this we say unto you by the word of the Lord, that we which are alive, and remain unto the coming of the Lord, shall not prevent them which are asleep. For the Lord Himself shall descend from heaven with a shout, with the voice of the archangel, and with the trump of God; and the dead in Christ shall rise first; then we which are alive and remain shall be caught up together with them in the clouds, to meet the Lord in the air; and so shall we ever be with the Lord" (I THESS. 4:15-17).

* * * * * * *

The second coming of Christ is the "Blessed Hope" and the inspiration of the Christian church. We are told in the Word of God to be prepared (Luke 12:31-48), to be waiting (Luke 12:36), to be ready (Matt. 24:44), to be faithful (Luke 12:42-44, to be patient (James 5:7-8), to be confident (I John 2:28), to be careful (Rom. 14:13), to be steadfast (I Cor. 15:57-58).

The person who is ready to meet his Lord is not content just to be ready and waiting, but he is busy telling others of Christ's coming, and he is helping them to get ready also. "Be ye therefore ready, for in such an hour as ye think not the Son of Man cometh." The Christian in this troubled world is giving thanks and rejoicing that he is ready. The being ready in this confused world is expressed in this quotation: "On a bough that swings, sits a bird that sings, because it has wings."

The second coming of Christ is a prominent theme throughout the New Testament. More is said about the second coming of Christ than is said about His first coming; and there are twenty times more references in the Old Testament about Christ's second coming than there are about His first coming. One in every thirty verses in the New Testament refers to Christ's return.

The second coming of Christ is the key that unlocks the Bible. The fact of the second coming is told by Jesus Himself (Matt. 24:6-27; Matt. 25:31-32; John 14:2-3; John 21:22). It is told by the apostles (Rev. 1:7; I John 2:28; Jude 1:14-15; James 5:7; II Peter 1:16; Heb. 9:28; Phil. 3:20-21; Titus 2:13; I Cor. 11:26). Paul speaks of the Lord's return 50 times. Messengers from heaven also speak of this great event (Acts 1:10-11; Rev. 11:3-12). The return of Christ is the remedy for the present world chaos.

The truth found in the Word of God leads us, who are His children, to believe that the second coming of Christ is near at hand, even at the door. Most Bible students agree that nearly all signs which point to His return and which are prophesied in the Word of God, have been fulfilled.

When Jesus talked with His disciples, He said to them, "And when these things begin to come to pass, then look up and lift up your heads; for your redemption draweth nigh." He said also, "And then shall they see the Son of Man coming in a cloud with power and great glory" (Luke 21:27-28).

The disciples said to Jesus, "Tell us when shall these things be." "What shall be the sign of Thy coming?"

"What shall be the sign of the consummation of the age?" Only the Omniscient God could answer these questions; and He answered them in advance by prophecy.

These are the signs that are prophesied, and which immediately usher in the second coming of Christ. They match this age universally and exactly. A number of these signs are recorded in Matt. 24 and in Luke 21.

1. The present condition in the nations is like that just before the flood. "As it was in the days of Noah, so shall it be also in the days of the Son of Man" (Luke 17:26-30). Then, people were engrossed in material interests, and they forgot God. In the time of Noah, there was:

A. An increase in city population.

B. Progress in civilization.

C. Worshipping God as Creator, and not as Redeemer as accomplished through the cross of Jesus Christ.

D. Fellowship of the church with the world.

E. Changed law about women and marriage.

F. Demon possession.

G. Indifference of many preachers marked with but few conversions.

H. People lovers of mere pleasure rather than lovers of God.

I. Wickedness prevailing all over the world.

These conditions are now universal, as they were in the time of Noah.

2. Crime and lawlessness exists. Most crimes now are committed by young people. "In the last days perilous times shall come."

3. False Christs, apostasy in the church, cults, and doctrines of demons prevail (I Tim. 4:1).

4. Scoffers, worldly people, ridiculing the Bible, second-coming preachers called "obsolete".

5. Persecution and hatred both of Jew and of Christian Gentile.

6. Travel and knowledge. "Many shall run to and fro, and knowledge shall be increased." "Chariots shall be with flaming torches in the day of His preparation, and the fir tree shall be terribly shaken. The chariots shall rage in the streets, they shall jostle one against another in the broad ways: they shall seem like torches, they shall run like lightning" (Nahum 2:3-4). This refers to automobiles. It was prophesied over 2600 years ago.

Airplanes also are prophesied. "As birds flying, so will the Lord of hosts defend Jerusalem; defending also He will deliver it, and passing over He will preserve it" (Isa. 31:5). This was prophesied 2667 years before it happened in 1917 under the command of General Allenby.

Knowledge surely is increased by radio, by telephone, by telegraph, and the like. We are nearing the end.

7. Great wealth, yet much national debt and unemployment (James 1:5-8).

8. Social disturbances, economic distress, fear, financial trouble, taxes, strife, sickness. These precede Christ's second coming.

9. Wars, and peace planning. England is fighting, but she has a reconstruction commission preparing for peace. Still, war marches on.

10. Consolidations and unions, preparing for a superman, the anti-Christ.

11. Earthquakes, floods, pestilence, famines (Matt. 24:7). Earthquakes, in recent years, have become so numerous that men do not stop to count them. There is yet to be one of the greatest earthquakes (Zech. 14:4-8). There is now great famine in many places.

12. Revolutions and strikes. There is hatred over conditions as they exist today. There is general uprising among the people.

13. Dictatorship like that in the time of Nebuchadnezzar. Federations like at the start of the Old Roman Empire (Dan. 2:31-45).

14. The return of the Jews to Palestine. They have been returning without faith in their Messiah.

15. A church that is not considering the return of Christ. There is apostasy in the church. A very small number of people are looking for Christ's return (Luke 12:40). Behold, He is near at hand.

16. Signs in the heavens.

17. The true church of Jesus Christ is beginning to understand God's prophecies pertaining to the second coming of Christ. Prophecy is not now a closed book, as it has been in the past. The time of Christ's return therefore is near at hand. "Watch, therefore. Be ready."

The second coming of Christ is in two parts. Many students of the Bible become confused about the second coming of Christ because they do not realize this fact. The two stages are seven years apart.

The first stage of Christ's return is called the "Rapture." as shown on the Art Chart. Here, Christ comes *for* His church. The second stage is called the "Revelation," as shown on the Chart. Here Christ comes *with* His church, and with all His Hosts of Heaven to judge the nations, and to set up His kingdom on earth. The saints go at the time of the Rapture to be with Jesus. They cannot come with Him at the time of the "Revelation" unless at that time they are already with Him.

Christ's coming at the "Rapture" is a surprise. "Watch therefore, for ye know neither the day nor the hour when the Son of Man cometh." The saints are the body of Christ and the body cannot be broken. Scripture demands that the "Rapture" come before the tribulation period. The tribulation period is not for the church, the body of Christ. The church has no part in it (Luke 21: 36; II Peter 2:9).

The time space of seven years between the first stage and the second stage of Christ's coming is filled with events. On the earth will be the time of the tribulation, the time of "Jacob's trouble"; and in the heavens above will take place the judgment of the church at the "Judgment Seat of Christ" and the marriage feast of the Lamb. Then Christ will receive His kingdom. "Let us be glad and rejoice, and give honor to him: for the marriage of the Lamb is come, and his wife has made herself ready" (Rev. 19:7).

What is said about *how* Christ will come at the time of the "Rapture"? He will come with a "shout of victory"—A "shout" that will command the "Dead in Christ", and a "shout" which they can hear. He shall come with the voice of an archangel, so that those who are alive, and who are His, will detect His call. As the disciples on earth saw Jesus go, so will the church see Him come at the "Rapture."

He will come with the "trump of God", which is looked upon as a final call to the "dead in Christ," who have all heard His "shout," who have been separated from the "wicked dead," and who have been raised from their graves; and then at the same time as a final call to His living church, which will be ready and which will be changed in the twinkling of an eye. It is a call to the righteous and holy, both the quick and the dead, to leave the earth and to meet their Lord and Saviour in the air. The Holy Spirit, who has been with the church on earth since Pentecost, will go also.

The bodies of the "dead in Christ" will rise first. They are "called out" from among all the bodies of the dead. The rest of the dead, the bodies left in the grave at that time, are the "wicked dead." They do not hear the "shout" of Christ, because they do not know Him. They will remain dead in the grave, for they will not be raised until the second resurrection, which comes after the thousand years of the Millennium kingdom, and which leads up to the judgment of the "Great White Throne," the judgment of the "wicked dead." Read John 5:28-29: "marvel not at this, for the hour is coming in the which all that are in the grave shall hear his voice and shall come forth."

The raising of the "dead in Christ" out from among the wicked dead is like separating particles of choice steel from a great pile of rubbish outside of a steel mill. In order to separate the choice steel from the rubbish in the pile, a great magnet fastened to a huge steel crane is swung out over the mixed pile. The particles of steel feel the pull of the great magnet and they take the life of the magnet. They quickly push their way out from among the other particles in the pile. They rise then to meet the magnet, and they cling to the magnet in the air. With the magnet, they are swung back by the crane to their home in the foundry. Thus the "Rapture" will be the first stage of the second coming of Christ. "Beloved, our citizenship is in heaven."

Jesus Christ first came to earth as a babe, which event is called the First Advent of Christ. He came not to be ministered unto but to minister, and to give His life a ransom for many. He came to save the souls of men. He suffered bodily, and He went away bodily. The Second Advent of Christ will be bodily and personal. He will come then to save the bodies of men and women whose souls are saved.

Many teachers try to explain away the personal return of Christ, principally because they lack a knowledge and an understanding of God's Word. The second coming of Christ does not mean the death of the believer. It does not mean the descent of the Holy Spirit at Pentecost. It does not mean the conversion of the sinner. It does not mean the diffusion of Christianity. It does not mean the destruction of Jerusalem. It means just what Jesus said it meant: I, Jesus Christ, will come again and will receive you, both the "dead in Christ" and the living church, to be with me. The church is destined to play an important part in the program of God, for its members will reign with Christ.

To the born-again Christian, the second coming of Christ means that he will be like Jesus, that he will be with Him, that he will reign with Him.

To the down-trodden, Christ-rejecting, persecuted Jew, the return of Christ to the earth will mean his hope of a new life. The Jews will recognize Him then, and will accept Him as their Messiah. It will mean that the Jews will be restored to their own land in peace, and that they will become a nation again (Jer. 16:14-15; Isa. 43: 5-7; Acts 15:14-17). The waste places of Palestine will be inhabited and builded and tilled. All this prophecy has not yet been fulfilled.

To the Gentile nations, the return of Christ will mean the destruction of the present political world-system of which the devil is the prince (Dan. 2:34-35, Rev. 19:11). It will mean the end of wars, of labor troubles, and of subversive movements. It will mean the judgment of the nations (Matt. 25:31-46). It will mean the separation of the "sheep nations" from the "goat nations." It will mean the destruction of the "goat nations", and the survival and peace of the "sheep nations." The "sheep nations" will become righteous (Matt. 25:31-40, Micah 4:3-4, Isa. 2).

To the earth, the return of Christ will mean that it will no longer be cursed, and it shall yield its increase (Isaiah 35:1; Psalm 67:6).

Be ye therefore ready. "Eye hath not seen, nor ear heard, neither hath entered into the heart of man, the things which God hath prepared for them that love Him" (I Cor. 2:9).

CHAPTER XIX

THE TRIBULATION PERIOD

> "For then shall be great tribulation, such as was not
> since the beginning of the world to this time, no, nor ever
> shall be. And except those days should be shortened,
> there should be no flesh saved; but for the elect's sake,
> those days shall be shortened" (MATT. 24:21-22).

* * * * * * *

The tribulation period is a time of seven years immediately following the departure of the Church and the Holy Spirit from the earth. It extends from the Rapture to the Revelation of Jesus Christ (Jer. 30:3-7). It is the seventh week of Daniel (Dan. 9:27), and the day of the anti-Christ. The anti-Christ will be revealed after the Rapture, and he will become the absolute dictator of the world. This period will greatly affect the Jews and the Gentiles who are unsaved. What happens during the tribulation period is described in Rev. 6:1 to Rev. 19:21.

The removal of all true Christians from the earth will cause great consternation and confusion on the earth. People will look for the cause of this departure. The seven years of this tribulation period are divided into two parts of three and one-half years each. At the beginning of this period, which is characterized by the breaking of the seals (Rev. 6:1), the anti-Christ will be revealed, and he will make a covenant with the Jewish people. At the end of three and one-half years in this period, the anti-Christ breaks his covenant.

Satan, who is sometimes referred to as the great dragon, with all his angels, is cast out of the heavenlies. He has always been opposed to the work of God, and he does all he can to oppose God's chosen people. He directs his woes upon the Jews especially, because Christ was born of the Jewish race, and is elevated to a place of power. The anti-Christ is empowered by the Devil. The period of "Great Tribulation" is the last three and one-half years of the seven years. It is called the "Time of Jacob's Trouble."

A second beast rises up out of the sea. He is the false prophet. He does lying wonders. He blasphemes God, and causes the people to worship the first beast. He causes all people to receive a "mark," either in their forehead or in their right hand. He causes that no man can buy or sell without the mark of the beast. The anti-Christ is then acknowledged by the world as ruler, and he is worshipped as God.

The remnant of God's chosen people, Israel, shall be delivered from all these woes, and will go to a place prepared for them, that they may hide themselves for three and one-half years. This time will be shortened for the elect's sake.

This period is also a period of salvation. A body of 144,000 people of Israel are sealed. Another group called "the Blood-Washed Multitude" are saved during the "Great Tribulation," the last three and one-half years of this period. They are not the Church, but they have accepted the Saviour, after the Church has been taken up to be with Christ. All of these are the tribulation saints, martyrs of this bloody period. Their souls after their death are seen under the altar, as observed by John. These martyrs are those who have preached the "Gospel of the Kingdom," and have been persecuted unto death. They are the gleanings of the harvest. Their bodies are in the grave. There is a resurrection of these tribulation saints when they arise to help form the hosts of heaven. Scofield says that the innumerable host of Gentiles of Rev. 7:9, which are said to have come out of the "Great Tribulation," are not of the priesthood, the Church, but seem to stand somewhat in the relationship of the Levites to the priests under the Mosaic covenant (Rev. 7:15).

There is a scarlet woman who will appear riding on a beast which has seven heads and ten horns. She will be the apostate church at that time. She will later be destroyed.

The Jews will recognize that Christ is their Messiah, and that the Spirit of God has been poured out upon them. Three angel messengers then are sent forth to preach to the people. One preaches the "Everlasting Gospel" of judgment; another announces the "Fall of Babylon"; and the third preaches warnings of judgment to those who are tempted to worship the beast.

The period will end at the time of the battle of Armageddon on the plain of Megiddo. Christ shall return suddenly in glory with all the hosts of heaven. He will bring to an end the "Times of the Gentiles" and the tribulation period. He will come to judge the nations and to set up His Kingdom on earth.

On the Art Chart are pictured the seals, the trumpets, the vials, Satan and his hosts cast out of the heavenlies, the anti-Christ, the false prophet, the image, the scarlet woman, the altar, the "Little stone cut out without hands," Armageddon, the Revelation, and the Mount of Olives.

This kingdom of the anti-Christ on earth, which is set up during the tribulation period, is a counterfeit kingdom. The trinity of that kingdom is the Anti-Father who is Satan, the dragon; the Anti-Son, who is the first beast, the anti-Christ; and the Anti-Spirit, who is the second beast, the false prophet.

In the prayer Jesus taught His disciples, when they prayed, "Thy Kingdom Come," they did not pray for this counterfeit kingdom, but they prayed for the real kingdom of Christ which follows the tribulation period and the Revelation of Christ.

11753

At the conclusion of the tribulation period, Christ will set up His kingdom, and the Jews will accept their king. Satan will be bound and cast into the "bottomless pit" for 1000 years. The anti-Christ and the false prophet will be cast into the "Lake of Fire." Christ will judge the nations. Here again is the close of another period in which God tests man. It is a period in the conflict of the ages, between God and Satan, when Satan turns loose all the fury and power of his evil purposes.

A study of the Revelation will disclose the details of the work of the angels, the seals, the trumpets, and the vials (Rev. 6-8). Satan knows that he is in the last round of his losing conflict-of-the-ages with Christ. Again, in this time of trouble, the "Grace of God" is manifested, and the people who obey God will be saved. We are reminded of God's message, "He that endureth to the end shall be saved". "Be thou faithful unto death and I will give you a Crown of Life" (Rev. 2:10).

Chapter XX

THE ROMAN EMPIRE—THE NORTHERN
CONFEDERACY

"And the ten horns which thou sawest are ten kings,
which have received no kingdom as yet; but receive
power as kings one hour with the beast . . . These shall
make war with the Lamb and the Lamb shall overcome
them, for He is Lord of lords and King of kings" (Rev.
17:12-16).

* * * * * * *

In the time of Daniel, over 2500 years ago, and during
the Babylonian captivity, our Lord sent a dream to
Nebuchadnezzar, the king of Babylon. This dream
pictured the image of a man composed of different kinds
of metal. The interpretation of the dream, as revealed
by God to Daniel, told of the existence, development and
strength of the coming world empires.

The Roman Empire, as a world power, was represented by the legs, the feet, and the toes of the image.
The Roman Empire was destroyed and ceased to exist
before all the prophecies, as revealed in the image dream,
were fulfilled, or before the history of the Roman Empire
reached the toe part of the image. Students of Bible
prophecy, therefore, have reason to believe that the
Roman Empire is to be revived in order to fulfill
prophecy, and that this revival will be ushered in at
the time of the tribulation period.

The ten-kingdom part of the Roman Empire, which is
the last stage of its existence, is represented by the ten
toes of the image dream (Dan. 2 and 7). It is represented in the same manner by the ten horns of the
terrible beast of the vision of Daniel, and by the ten
horns of the beast of the vision of John on Patmos (Rev.

17:12). The Bible says that the ten kingdoms of the image dream were broken in pieces by "a stone cut out without hands" falling from heaven. This "stone" is Christ Himself, "the stone of Israel" (Gen. 49:24; Dan. 2:34-35; Dan. 2:44-45). "And the stone that smote the image became a great mountain and filled the whole earth." "God hath made known to the king what shall come to pass hereafter: and the dream is certain, and the interpretation thereof sure."

The Gentile nations of today are being shaken, pushed about and changed. We read startling articles about these changes in the daily newspapers and in the magazines; and we hear about them over the radio and from the platform. Bible students are watching with keen interest all of these changes that are taking place among nations; for prophecy is being fulfilled, and they know what to expect.

God used Nebuchadnezzar, the king of Babylon, an evil leader of a Gentile nation, to subdue weaker nations and to develop a powerful world empire (Dan. 2:37-38). God, in the same way, is using evil leaders today to subdue nations and to draw to a close the present age, the age of grace. Dictators of iron are now breaking up nations of clay and forcing them into submission. They are attempting to form leagues of nations. They are trying to become world conquerors. Things that have seemed to be impossible with man are now happening at the command of God. The Bible tells of two federations of nations yet to be formed, the Revived Roman Empire and the Northern Confederacy. Newspapers of today are unconsciously picturing the trend of nations toward the development of these two great federations.

The development of Italy toward becoming a powerful nation was started at the time of the last world war. Mussolini has been building Italy after the plan of the Caesars. He believes in the resurrection of the Roman

Empire.   He announced the Revival of the Roman Empire on May 9, 1936, and is now dating the official papers of Italy from 1927 R. R. E. which is the date he marched into Rome.   The papacy has become a temporal power, and the woman arrayed in purple and scarlet and riding on a beast with seven heads and ten horns, is regaining more temporal power (Rev. 17:1).

God will use the antichrist, the beast, who is thought to spring up out of some part of the Revived Roman Empire, and who is an evil man, to carry out His plan of conquest among the weaker nations, and to form a federation of nations in the tribulation period.   We do not know the leader who will be the antichrist.   Mussolini is fast preparing the time and the conditions in which the antichrist will be revealed.

The Jewish people do not as a whole receive Jesus, the real Christ, as their Messiah, for only a very few Jews are being converted now; but they will receive Him at the "Time of Jacob's trouble," when they will see Him as the one whom they have crucified.

When the antichrist is revealed after the rapture, however, the Jews will receive him instead of Christ.   The antichrist, at the beginning of the tribulation period, will make a covenant with the Jews.   He will break this covenant after three and one-half years.

Present-day dictators now are pressing forward in a strange and remarkable way.   What a shock it will be to many who are left behind at the rapture, when they discover that the saved people who were ready to meet their Lord have been caught up, and that they who remain are to be ruled by the antichrist.

This dictator will increase his activities rapidly during the tribulation period after he breaks his covenant with the Jews.   He will carry his conquests into Egypt (Dan. 11:42-43).   This will be the start of his last campaign. "He will stretch forth his hand also upon the countries; and the land of Egypt will not escape. But he shall have power over the treasures of gold and silver, and over all the precious things of Egypt: and the Libyans and the Ethiopians shall be at his steps" (Dan. 11: 42-43). The kings of the South will come against him, and the beast will conquer. He will conquer all of the Mediterranean countries except Edom, Moab, and Ammon (Dan. 11:41). These nations will be a place of refuge for the remnant of the Jews.

The Northern Confederacy also is preparing for conquest while the best of the Roman federation is conquering around the Mediterranean Sea with his eye on Palestine. Russia and Germany, as well as all the other countries of the North, also have their eyes on Palestine.

The Northern Confederacy is described in Ezek. 38: 8-9. "In the latter years thou shalt come into the land that is brought from the sword, and is gathered out of many people, against the mountains of Israel, which have been always waste: but it is brought forth out of the nations, and they shall dwell safely all of them. Thou shalt ascend and come like a storm, thou shalt be like a cloud to cover the land, thou and all thy bands, and many people with thee."

During recent years, Israel has been going back into her own land after being scattered among the nations. Read Ezek. 36, 37, 38. Gen. 10 gives the origin of the nations mentioned in Ezekiel, as Magog, Rosh, Meshech, Tubal, Togarmah, and Gomar.

The antichrist will be troubled by tidings out of the East and out of the North. With his federation of ten nations, he will meet the Northern Confederacy, with Gog as their head, in the valley of Esdralon. Both of these confederations will seek the wealth of Palestine. The antichrist will be the conqueror. He will become the head of the armies of all nations. This will lead him to the battle of Armageddon, to war against God's chosen people, the Jews. This war therefore will be fought by the combined armies of the Gentile nations under the leadership of the antichrist against the Jews. Then will occur the Revelation of Jesus Christ as the rider of the white horse from heaven. The result of Christ's coming on His white horse from heaven to battle against the antichrist will be that the hosts of the antichrist will be slaughtered in great numbers. The dead will be buried in the Valley of Hammon-Gog. The house of Israel will be seven months burying the dead of the armies of the antichrist. "And I saw the beast, and the kings of the earth, and their armies, gathered together to make war against him that sat on the horse, and against his army. And the beast was taken, and with him the false prophet that wrought miracles before him, with which he deceived them that had received the mark of the beast, and them that worshipped his image. These both were cast alive into a lake of fire burning with brimstone. And the remnant were slain with the sword of him that sat upon the horse, which sword proceeded out of His mouth: and all the fowls were filled with their flesh" (Rev. 19:19-21).

Thus will end the power of the antichrist, the king of the Revived Roman Empire. Today men would do well to search the Scriptures and to understand what God says about the future course of the Gentile nations. Christ will come with all His hosts of heaven, at the time of His revelation, to the Mount of Olives, to put a stop to the work of the antichrist, to judge the nations and to usher in His Kingdom.

Chapter XXI

THE JUDGMENTS

"There is, therefore, now no condemnation to them which are in Christ Jesus, who walk not after the flesh but after the spirit. For the law of the Spirit of life in Christ Jesus hath made me free from the law of sin and death" (Rom. 8:1-2).

* * * * * * *

A judgment is defined as a disaster or affliction, and is regarded as a punishment for sin. Seven judgments, as recorded in the Bible, are shown on the Art Chart. They are named at the bottom of the Chart and are located by number.

The Holy Spirit reveals to the believer, as he studies the Word of God, that there is more than one resurrection from the dead, and that there are several judgments which are entirely different from each other as to time, place, purpose, and outcome. Many preachers and teachers try to explain, however, that there is one general resurrection followed by one general judgment.

The seven judgments herein described are the judgment of the believer's sins by Jesus Christ Himself on the cross, the result of which is salvation; the judgment of the believer's self by himself here on earth, the result of which is sanctification; the judgment of the believer's works by Christ, the result of which is compensation; the judgment of the Jewish people here on earth by the Lord God, the result of which is restoration; the judgment of the nations on earth by the Son of Man, the result of which is separation; the judgment of the Fallen Angels in the air by the Saints, the result of which is condemnation; and the judgment of the wicked dead in heaven before God, the result of which is damnation.

These judgments happen, as you will notice, in different places. Some are on the earth, some are in the air, and one is in heaven. There are also three different thrones mentioned. One throne is called the "Judgment Seat of Christ," where Christ will be the judge of the believer's works (Rom. 14:10). Another throne on earth is called the "Throne of His Glory," where will take place the "Judgment of the Nations" (Matt. 25:31-32). And another throne is called the "Great White Throne," where will be held before God the "Judgment of the Wicked Dead" (Rev. 20:11-12).

JUDGMENT No. 1—FOR THE BELIEVER'S SINS

This judgment took place at the "Cross of Jesus Christ," where Christ paid the penalty of the broken law for us as sinners. This judgment is past. Christ hath redeemed us from the curse of the law, being made a curse for us (Gal. 3:13). He took upon Himself on the cross the guilt of our sins. So great was His love for us that He voluntarily gave His life that we might escape the supreme penalty of the law, which is death.

Let us rejoice and be glad and praise Jesus Christ, who hath redeemed us from this judgment and hath given us, who are His, Eternal Life. Paul said, "Believe on the Lord Jesus Christ, and thou shalt be saved and thy house." Jesus said, "He that heareth my word, and believeth on him that sent me, HATH everlasting life, and shall not come into condemnation, but IS PASSED from death unto life (John 5:24).

JUDGMENT No. 2—FOR THE BELIEVER'S SELF

This judgment is for the believer's self. The judge is the believer himself. The believer, as a child of God, has accepted the atonement of Jesus Christ, has been born again, and has received a spiritual nature. This nature does not take the place of his "Old Adamic Nature," but has been added to it as a new nature. Therefore the believer possesses a dual nature. These two natures strive the one against the other.

In this judgment, the Christian must judge himself each day and be guided by the Holy Spirit. That part of the dual nature of a Christian that is fed most predominates. Read I Cor. 11:28-34, and Romans 14:13. Self-judgment is more the believer's moral condemnation of himself for allowing his own ways and habits, than it is his condemnation of those ways and habits. If self-judgment is neglected, then the Lord judges, and the result is chastisement, but not condemnation. "But when we are judged, we are chastened of the Lord, that we should not be condemned with the world."

The Spiritual nature grows when it is freely led by the Holy Spirit. Growth is sustained by the study of the Word of God, by obedience to God, by Christian service and fellowship, and by prayer and praise.

The fleshly nature predominates when man is more concerned about what people think of him than he is about what God thinks of him. By striving to please people, he becomes proud and selfish, and thereby sinful. God can and does punish those who sin (Heb. 12:3-12). No disobedience, however small, goes unpunished. "If we confess our sins, He is faithful and just to forgive us our sins, and to cleanse us from all unrighteousness" (I John 1:9). When we judge ourselves aright, the Spiritual nature becomes master of the fleshly nature. "Happy is he that condemneth not himself in the thing that he alloweth" (Rom. 14:22).

Judgment No. 3—For the Believer's Works

This judgment and all the remaining four judgments are in the future. This judgment is for the saved ones only, for the Church of Jesus Christ, and it follows the Church Age. It takes place in the air at the "Judgment Seat of Christ," where Christ is the judge (I Thess. 4:17; I Cor.

4:5). It is pictured at the top of the Art Chart, following the Rapture. It is not a judgment for sin, but it is a judgment for the believer's works. We, the believers, must all appear before the "Judgment Seat of Christ" (II Cor. 5:10; I Cor. 3:8-14; Matt. 10:42; Matt. 16:27; Luke 19:17; I Cor. 9:24-25; II Tim. 4:8; Rev. 22:12).

All of our works will be tried as by fire. All of the "dead works" of the believer are represented at the "Judgment Seat of Christ" as "hay and stubble," and all these will be burned and lost. Our opinions are worthless, for without Christ we can do nothing. Some people who now hold high positions in the church on earth may be the least in the Kingdom of Heaven. The test will be made on how we have used our opportunities to witness for Christ and to win others for Him here on earth, according to our ability, position, wealth and sacrifice. God and the individual can determine what to do, and how to do it.

This judgment of the believer's works brings to the believer either "loss" or "reward." The believer's rewards are described in the next chapter.

JUDGMENT NO. 4—FOR THE JEWS

This judgment is called "The Time of Jacob's Trouble" (Jer. 30:4-7; Dan. 12:1). It takes place on the earth after the Jews have returned to Palestine, and after the "Fullness of the Gentiles." The cause of this judgment is very evident. The Jews, as a people, have disobeyed God. They have rejected Him (I Sam. 8:7); they have rejected Jesus Christ (Luke 23:18); and they have rejected the Holy Spirit (Acts 7:51; Acts 7:54-60). Therefore, they have refused to accept the "Trinity of the Godhead."

As a punishment, the Jews have been scattered among all nations. They are now going back to their own land unconverted. They are to be judged after the close of the Age of Grace and during the Tribulation Period, when the anti-Christ is on earth. They will be cast into

God's "melting pot." At the Revelation of Jesus Christ, the Jewish Nation will be restored (Isa. 56:8).

JUDGMENT NO. 5—FOR THE NATIONS

At the time of this judgment, the Church will have been judged in the air, and the Jews will have been judged on the earth. The "Times of the Gentiles" will have ceased. The Nations are now at the Revelation of Jesus Christ at the end of the tribulation period, to be judged for their treatment of "His Brethren," the Jews (Joel 3:2). Christ with His Church will be the judge. No "books" will be opened at this judgment.

As a result of this judgment, the "Sheep Nations" will inherit a kingdom, the Millennium Kingdom, and they will be among the Saved Nations of the New Earth (Rev. 21: 24). The "Goat Nations" will be cast into everlasting fire, and they will be destroyed as nations. This judgment is not for individuals, it is for nations. "For behold, in those days, and in that time, when I shall bring again the captivity of Judah and Jerusalem, I will also gather all nations, and will bring them down into the Valley of Jehoshaphat, and will plead with them there for my people and for my heritage, Israel, whom they have scattered among the nations, and parted my land" (Joel 3:1-2).

JUDGMENT NO. 6—FOR THE FALLEN ANGELS

"And the angels which kept not their own estate, but left their own habitation, He hath reserved in everlasting chains under darkness unto the judgment of the "Great Day" (Jude 1:6). This is the Day of the Lord (Isa. 2:9-22).

Satan will meet his doom after the one thousand years of the Kingdom Age, preceding the Judgment of the Great White Throne of Rev. 20:11-15. At this time other fallen angels are to be judged (II Peter 2:4). "God spared not the fallen angels that sinned, but cast them down to hell, and delivered them into chains of darkness to be reserved for judgment."

Michael, the archangel, said when contending with the Devil, "The Lord rebuke thee" (Jude 1:9). In Rev. 20:10 we find these words, "And the devil that deceived them was cast into the lake of fire and brimstone, where the beast and the false prophet are, and shall be tormented day and night for ever and ever."

JUDGMENT NO. 7—FOR THE WICKED DEAD

"But the rest of the dead lived not again until the thousand years were finished." These dead are the wicked dead, who were not a part of the First Resurrection, but whose bodies wait in the grave and whose souls remain in hades, the place appointed for the souls of the wicked dead, until the Second Resurrection.

"And I saw a Great White Throne and him that sat upon it, from whose face the earth and the heavens fled away, and there was found no place for them."

"And I saw the dead, small and great, stand before God; and the books were open; and another book was open which is the Book of Life; and the dead were judged out of those things which were written in the books, according to their works."

We find, therefore, that there is a resurrection of the wicked dead, which is the Second Resurrection, when the wicked dead will appear before the Great White Throne to be judged for their works. The judge is God. Then the earth will be renovated by fire.

"And whosoever was not found written in the Book of Life was cast into the lake of fire" (Rev. 20:11-15). "And death and hell were cast into the lake of fire. This is the second death." "Blessed and holy is he that hath part in the First Resurrection, on such the Second Death hath no power" (Rev. 20:5, 6).

Chapter XXII

THE CROWNS

"Behold, I come quickly: hold that fast which thou hast, that no man take thy crown" (Rev. 3:11).

* * * * * * *

At the Judgment Seat of Christ, where the believer will be judged for his "works," Christ will give crowns to those who deserve rewards. The believer's "works" will be tested as by fire. Some works will be burned, causing the believer to suffer loss, while other works will endure, for which the believer will receive a reward. It will be a "crowning day" for those who will receive rewards. The New Testament speaks of five crowns.

THE CROWN OF LIFE—James 1:12; Rev. 2:10

The "crown of Life" is the "martyr's" crown. It is mentioned twice in the Scriptures. It will be given to those who suffer persecution for Christ's sake. "Be thou faithful unto death, and I will give thee a Crown of Life."

THE CROWN OF GLORY—I Peter 5:2-4

This is the "Elder's or Pastor's" crown. It will be for those who have faithfully taught Christ's teachings because of their love for Christ.

THE CROWN OF REJOICING—I Thess. 2:19-20

This is the "soul-winner's" crown. It will be given to those who have won souls for the Lord Jesus Christ. It will be a great reward just to see those whom we have won.

May we do and say only that which can be used to save many souls, without hope of personal reward or gratitude. Some Christians may drive sinful men away

113

from Christ because of their attitude toward those in sin, for the simple reason that they show on their faces their own condemnation of the sinner. "Judge not that ye be not judged." Every Christian should rejoice continually for his own salvation. The first thing a soul-winner should cultivate is a cheerful countenance (II Tim. 2: 24-26) that he may show to the unconverted, with great joy, the love of Jesus Christ.

The Crown of Righteousness—II Tim. 4:8

This crown is for those who are looking for the appearing of Christ. It will be given on the day of His appearing. There are a great many people today who do not believe in the personal return of Christ in spite of the fact that Jesus said "I will come again." He will come as He went. "Every man that hath this hope in him purifieth himself, even as he is pure" (I John 3:3).

The Crown Incorruptible—I Cor. 9:25-27

This crown is the Victor's crown. It is for those who "keep under the body." It is for those who do not yield to fleshly lusts, for those who do not let worldly amusements and pleasures interrupt or interfere with God's work. The greatest battles of life are fought in the heart. Let us accept the help of Jesus, and He will win our battles for us. Let us win a Victor's crown. "What a friend we have in Jesus."

Chapter XXIII

THE KINGDOM AGE

"The Lord God shall give unto Him, (Jesus), the throne of his father David. And he shall reign over the house of Jacob for ever; and of his kingdom there shall be no end" (LUKE 1:32, 33).

* * * * * * *

The God of heaven will set up a kingdom. It will come suddenly, when the "Stone cut out without hands" will smite the Gentile nations. There is no gradual conversion of the world and no process of evolution to make things perfect. Jesus Christ will smite the nations and will judge them. Then He will set up His kingdom on the earth. It will be a literal, tangible, visible kingdom. It will be the first and only universal kingdom. It will take the place of all governments and nations. "The kingdoms of this world are become the kingdoms of our Lord and of His Christ" (Rev. 11:15).

Christ will reign in person on the earth on the throne of His Father, David. His kingdom will be eternal. He will be assisted by the saints of the first resurrection. The seat of Christ's government will be at Jerusalem. At the name of Jesus every knee shall bow, of things in heaven and things in earth and things under the earth (Phil. 2:10). Israel will be saved and will become the head of the nations.

This millennium age extends from the Revelation of Jesus Christ to the setting up of the "Great White Throne." There will be 1000 years of rest and blessing under the direct supervision of Christ as King. It will be a period of glorious expansion, of universal prosperity. The earth will yield her increase.

However, the innate evil of man's nature will still remain. There will be professors and possessors, unchanged hearts and changed hearts. People will yield to the King in obedience during the millennium age, but evil will be present in the hearts of men although Satan will be absent. Sin, when it shows itself, will be immediately suppressed.

This millennial kingdom, therefore, will not be a perfect kingdom, although there will be great blessing and prosperity. God's curse upon the physical universe will be removed (Isa. 55:13). Sin will still be in evidence, as revealed by the revolt of the people led by Satan at the close of the age. Sin and death must be destroyed.

Satan will be loosed, after being chained in the bottomless pit for the millennium age, a period of 1000 years. He will lead a revolt against God. People will have to make their choice between God and Satan.

"When the thousand years are expired, Satan shall be loosed out of his prison, and shall go out to deceive the nations which are in the four corners of the earth, Gog and Magog, to gather them together to the war; the number of whom is as the sands of the sea; and they went up over the breadth of the earth, and compassed the camp of the saints about and the beloved city." The names Gog and Magog must not be confused with Gog and Magog of Ezekiel 38 and 39. The prophecy of Ezekiel takes place before the millennium, while the scene in Revelation 20:7, 8 is fulfilled after the 1000 year reign.

Men will flock in multitudes to Satan in revolt against God. The result will be that all of the rebels will be destroyed by fire from heaven, and Satan will be cast into the Lake of Fire. Then the Great White Throne will be set up for the judgment of sinners only. The wicked dead will be cast into the Lake of Fire, which is the second death. Both death, the fruit of sin, and Hell, the abode of lost souls and spirits, which were brought into existence by Satan, will be destroyed. The lost who were in Hades will be sent to their eternal abode in the Lake of Fire.

The millennium follows an unparalleled period of confusion and tribulation. It ends with a universal revolt and war which will be quickly stopped by fire from heaven (Rev. 20:9).

CHAPTER XXIV

A NEW HEAVEN AND A NEW EARTH

"And I saw a new heaven and a new earth; for the first heaven and the first earth were passed away; and there was no more sea. And I, John, saw the Holy City, new Jerusalem, coming down from God out of heaven, prepared as a bride adorned for her husband. And I heard a great voice out of heaven saying, Behold, the tabernacle of God is with men, and he will dwell with them, and they shall be his people; and God himself shall be with them and be their God" (REV. 21:1-3).

* * * * * * *

A New Heaven and a New Earth are pictured on the Art Chart at the very end of the diagram. The full purpose of God will be realized in a perfect age when man has been restored, the earth has been renewed, Satan and sin have been defeated, death and hell have been vanquished, and Christ has been crowned King of kings and Lord of lords.

Then Christ will have finished His reign during the Millennial age, and will have put all enemies under His feet. He will have finished the work that He was given to do as the Son of Man. In that perfect and eternal age, Christ will surrender the Kingdom to God, that God may be "All in All." The divine "Godhead" will act again as a "Unity."

The meaning of "a New Heaven and a New Earth" is extremely interesting and important. Bible students differ in their interpretation and meaning of this.

The verse of Scripture at the beginning of this chapter would lead us to believe that the earth, as a planet, and the heavens surrounding the earth, will be completely destroyed by fire. A closer study, however, does not seem to reveal total destruction.

The word "New," in this verse, does not appear to mean something just coming into existence. It appears to mean something already in existence becoming reconditioned, renovated, or physically transformed by fire. This latter meaning of the word "New" is accepted by most Bible students.

The Greek word "Cosmos" as used in this verse by the apostle, means "land surface," and the Greek word "Parerchomia" means to pass "from one condition to another." Reference to these two Greek words, therefore, leads one to believe that the exterior surface of the earth will be completely changed. All the curse that Satan and sin have brought upon the surface of the earth will be destroyed, and the atmosphere around the earth will be purged from evil and destructive things; but the framework or foundation of the earth will remain. The old creation of heaven and earth must be purified from the stain of sin (II Peter 3:5-15).

It seems quite incredible that the present earth, which God first created, will become extinct; for the reason that the primitive earth, which in prehistoric times was made void by Satan, was restored again by God. This same earth, which was cursed before the flood by sinful things and by sinful people, was purged of evil people by the flood which covered the earth, so that a new people under Noah was started. In a similar way, it would seem that the surface of this earth, which in the time of Adam and Eve in the garden of Eden, was pure for innocent man, must be cleansed from sin by fire, by the destruction of organic substance on the earth, and of all combustible matter around the earth, so that the earth again will be free from sin, and will become a fit material dwelling place for the resurrected saints, those who have been redeemed from sin and a sinful earth.

The natural interpretation of much of the Scriptural teaching about the earth is that this earth will be the final abode of the redeemed people. The earth will be made perfect for the habitation of the saints in the kingdom of God. The saints will inhabit the earth. In Genesis there is described an earthly paradise lost, with a curse inflicted; while in the Revelation there is described the curse removed by fire and by judgment, and an earthly paradise restored. "One generation passeth away and another generation cometh, but the earth abideth forever" (Ecc. 1:4).

The Bible speaks of the eternal home of the glorified beings below on a glorified earth. The glorified will spend eternity here on earth.

The Millennium will not be a perfect age, for at that time there will be conflict within some men. In the "New Heaven and the New Earth" there will be no conflict of forces. There will be no pain, no sickness, no sorrow, no sighing, and no crying. Christ will have triumphed over sin and death. Christ will have surrendered the glorious kingdom to God. All people will depend upon God and the Lamb. All things celestial and terrestrial will be subject to the Son of God.

The chasm between heaven and earth will be bridged. The tabernacle of God will be with man, so that separation of man from God will be at an end. God's servants will see Him, and will serve Him with gladness. There will be no night there, for God Himself will be the light of the universe.

There will be a new city, a Holy City, the New Jerusalem, which will come down out of heaven, prepared as a bride adorned for her husband. It will have no temple, for the Lord God Almighty and the Lamb will be the temple of it. Then the tabernacle of God will be with men.

CHAPTER XXV

SEARCH THE SCRIPTURES—PRAY—AND TRUST GOD

> "Search the scriptures; for in them ye think ye have
> eternal life; and they are they which testify of me"
> (JOHN 5:39).

* * * * * * *

A knowledge of the Bible is, as revealed by God Himself, an essential part of the true education of any person. In fact, no one can be called truly educated who has not attained such knowledge. No other culture or training received from any institution of elementary or of higher education can be a proper substitute for a knowledge of the Word of God as revealed by the Holy Spirit.

With an understanding of the Bible revealed to us by the Holy Spirit, we as Christians may know God's plan for the past ages; we may know God's plan of salvation for us now through the blood of Jesus Christ; and we should know His prophetic plan for the future, for His church and for the world. We should know the full purpose of God for the earth upon which we live. The Bible makes plain that evangelism is the foundation principle of Christianity. All truly born-again believers today are interested in the salvation of the lost, and in the work of the Church of Jesus Christ. The Gospel of Jesus Christ is the power of God unto salvation to all who believe.

Christians, in their work of evangelism, will be wise to base their appeal to the unsaved to accept Christ as their Saviour and Redeemer on the authority of the written Word of God. The reason is that the Gospel message, as read from the written Word of God, is always empowered by the Holy Spirit, and the Holy Spirit always works effectively and permanently to meet human needs.

On the contrary, man's message is prone to be ineffective and to fail, because man is so changeable and human. Dwight L. Moody said that he never knew of a person being converted to Christ without some influence of the written Word of God.

A powerful force is being unloosed by the world-wide distribution of the Bible. When an unsaved person is given the written Word of God, it is his, and in his possession, to read. Although he may not be intensely interested in its message at first, he is less likely to throw it away because it is his. He can take it with him, and read it when alone, while unmolested, in his own room, when the sounds of the world have died out in his soul. When a person is alone with the Bible, this is often the time when the Holy Spirit does His work of convincing the unsaved of his sin. When alone with the Bible, a man can more clearly hear the whisperings of God, which are able to lead to the regeneration of human life. The Holy Spirit at times seems to magnify certain verses in print so that they stand out on the page with special power and persuasion.

Truly effective evangelism needs a combined impression which involves both the eye and the ear. This double impression will more readily bring to the unsaved a conviction of sin, a repentance in the heart, and a realization of the need of Christ as Saviour, which leads to salvation. The effect of visual art, in causing a better understanding of the Scriptures on the part of the student, has influenced the creation of the Beckwith Art Chart of Bible History and Prophecy.

God can help a man, through His written Word and by the help of the Holy Spirit, to take the forces that are arrayed against him and make them stepping stones to the very gates of heaven and into the presence of the living God. God can bend all of these contrary forces for man's good. Moreover, God can take the life crushed by pain and sorrow and make it into a harp whose music shall be all praise. The Almighty God can make us stronger than our circumstances.

Therefore, read the Bible. Let us read it to be wise, let us believe it to be safe, and let us practice it to be holy. We should persuade others to read, that they may come to a knowledge of the truth and be saved.

The story is told of a little boy who had heard much of the kindness of his king. He developed such a desire to see that kind king that one day he left his home to seek the ruler. The boy went some distance until he came to the iron gateway that led to the courtyard of the palace of the king. He started to enter through the gateway, but a strong guard stopped him and said, "My boy you cannot enter here, for this entrance leads to the palace of the king. You are a stranger. What do you want?" The boy answered, "Sir, I know that this is the gateway that leads to the palace of the king. I want to enter, for I wish to see him." When refused admittance, the boy was sad and disappointed. He turned aside, sat down on a nearby stone, and began to cry. Soon another boy came along. He saw the lad sitting on the stone, crying, so he went over to him. Putting his hand on the weeping boy's shoulder, he said, "Hello, what is the trouble? Why are you crying?" The boy looked up and told his new friend of his disappointment, how he had come a long distance to see the king about whom he had heard so much, and how, when he had arrived at the gateway that led to the palace of the king, the guard would not allow him to enter because he was a stranger.

The new friend replied, "Is that the reason why you are sad? Do you really want to see the king? Then come with me, and I will take you in through these gates, for I am the King's son and he is my father." Joyfully, the little stranger accompanied the son to see the King. In the same way our Christ, the Son of God, will take us who are saved into the presence of His Father, the King of the universe.

Jesus said, "I am the way, the truth, and the life: no man cometh unto the Father but by me." "There is none other name under heaven given among men whereby we must be saved."

God wants men to know His Word, the Holy Scriptures. He does not especially want great men, but He does want humble and faithful men who dare to prove the greatness of their God.

"The Lord thy God in the midst of thee is mighty."

Jesus said to His disciples, "Follow Me, and I will make you—

> "Make you speak my words with power,
> Make you helpful every hour,
> Make you loving, truthful, godly,
> Make you channels of my mercy,
> Make you what you cannot be,
> Make you even like to Me."

"More things are wrought by prayer than this world dreams of." Prayer connects one with the Divine battery of life and power. No physical agency can hinder the creative power of prayer. The men who have done the most for God have been early in prayer. We must talk with God in prayer in the name of Jesus Christ.

Every day, the Christian must receive the renewing of the Holy Spirit. He must not attempt to face the day until he has first faced God. It is there, with God alone, that he mounts up on top of his load, and rests in Him.

In every circumstance that aims to pain you, the sting will go as you learn to see Jesus in everything. Your safety lies in letting Jesus fight your battles for you. Faith that goes forward triumphs.

I pray that the last chapter of your book of life, in this age of grace, may be such that you can say with Paul,—"I have fought a good fight, I have finished my course, I have kept the faith."

"I pray God your whole spirit, soul, and body be preserved blameless unto the coming of our Lord Jesus Christ" (I Thess. 5:23).

> "It matters not how the battle goes,
> The day how long;
> *Faint not! Fight on!*
> Tomorrow comes the song."

PRINTED IN THE UNITED STATES OF AMERICA

INDEX